FREE AT LAST

A History of the
Civil Rights Movement
and Those Who Died
in the Struggle

SARA BULLARD

INTRODUCTION BY
JULIAN BOND

OXFORD UNIVERSITY PRESS
NEW YORK

FRANKLIN PIERCE COLLEGE
LIBRARY
RINDGE, NEW HAMPSHIRE

Oxford University Press

Oxford   New York   Toronto
Delhi   Bombay   Calcutta
Madras   Karachi
Kuala Lumpur   Singapore
Hong Kong   Tokyo
Nairobi   Dar es Salaam
Cape Town   Melbourne
Auckland   Madrid

and associated companies in

Berlin   Ibadan

Copyright © 1993 by The Southern
Poverty Law Center

Published by
Oxford University Press, Inc.,
200 Madison Avenue,
New York, New York 10016

Oxford is a registered trademark of
Oxford University Press

All rights reserved.
No part of this publication
may be reproduced,
stored in a retrieval system,
or transmitted,
in any form or by any means,
electronic, mechanical,
photocopying, recording,
or otherwise,
without the prior
permission of
Oxford University Press.

Library of Congress
Cataloging-in-Publication Data

Bullard, Sara.
    Free at last : a history of the Civil
Rights Movement and those who died in
the struggle / Sara Bullard : introduction
by Julian Bond.
    p. cm.
    Includes bibliographical references
and index.
    Summary: An illustrated history of
the civil rights movement, including a
timeline and profiles of forty people
who gave their lives in the movement.
    ISBN 0-19-508381-4
    1. Afro-Americans—Civil rights—
Juvenile literature. 2. Civil rights movement—United States—History—20th
century—Juvenile literature. 4. United
States—race relations—Juvenile literature. [1. Civil rights movement—History.
2. Afro-Americans—Civil rights. 3. Civil
rights workers. 4. Race relations.] I. Title.
    E185.61.B926 1993

323.1'196073—dc20

CIP   92-38174
AC

2 4 6 8 9 7 5 3 1

Printed in the United States of America
on acid-free paper

Acknowledgements

Consultants
Julian Bond, Morris Dees,
J. Richard Cohen,
Taylor Branch, Steve Fiffer

Senior Researcher
Joseph T. Roy Sr.

With Assistance from
Southern Regional Council, U.S. Library of Congress,
Mississippi and Alabama State Archives, Birmingham Public Library,
Center for the Study of Southern Culture at the University of Mississippi,
Martin Luther King Center for Nonviolent Social Change,
Cathy Lane, Nancy Britnell, Jeff Richburg, Charles Blevins, Barbara Blank,
and Members of the Civil Rights Memorial Advisory Committee.

Book Design by
Susan Hulme/Wright

Special thanks

To the many relatives and friends of those who died during the movement,
for providing us with valuable letters, photographs, documents and remembrances.

Originally published by Teaching Tolerance, the education project of
The Southern Poverty Law Center, Montgomery, AL. ©1989

Bulk copies of a magazine version of this publication
may be ordered for classroom use by writing to:
Teaching Tolerance,
400 Washington Ave.,
Montgomery, AL 36104

One day the South will recognize its real heroes.

—Martin Luther King Jr.,
in *Letter from Birmingham City Jail*

Contents

Introduction

The civil rights movement that swept the Southern states in the 1950s and 1960s affects the lives of all Americans today. Yet most people do not realize what the movement did for them.

Today we have many laws against discrimination, laws that were created in response to the movement. These laws are intended to protect not only black people; they prohibit discriminatory treatment because of age, gender, physical or mental disadvantage, religion, or foreign ancestry.

Julian Bond (center) at an Atlanta government hearing in 1963.

And we all live in a country that is coming to acknowledge that discrimination is wrong.

The struggle of black Americans against discrimination is as old as the United States itself. It began when slavery was legal throughout the land.

I joined the modern civil rights struggle as a twenty-year-old college student. Many of the people I worked with became a part of the movement during their teenage years. A few were still in elementary school.

There was one distinguishing feature of this movement. Its participants and leaders ranged from ministers and students to farm workers and laborers. It was truly a democratic movement—anyone who would adhere to the movement's tactics and who believed in its goals was welcome. Anyone could play a part, and thousands — of all ages and races— did. Most of their names will never be known.

When I was a college student in Atlanta in 1960, black Atlantans could not eat at downtown lunch counters or try on clothes in department stores, attend most schools, or work at well-paying jobs.

Outside Atlanta, and elsewhere in the South, blacks who dared to try to register to vote were met by violence; sometimes even by death.

But many had struggled quietly for years to win their basic Constitutional rights.

In 1955, at the age of fifteen, I had been frightened by the murder of Emmett Till in Mississippi. Till was only one year younger than I was. He had done nothing wrong; he had merely dared to speak to a white woman. I was afraid someone might try to kill me too because of the color of my skin.

Later that year, I eagerly watched news reports of the bus boycott 150 miles away in Montgomery, Alabama, led by a young minister named Martin Luther King, Jr., who had graduated from my college just a few years before. When Montgomery's 50,000 blacks walked to work and school for more than a year, rather than sit in the back of segregated buses, I was filled with pride.

And when nine brave black teenagers— most of them close to my age— walked through screaming mobs to integrate Central High School in Little Rock, Arkansas, in 1957, I wondered if I could be as brave as they had been.

When a fellow student approached me to ask if I would join in planning non-violent demonstrations against Atlanta's segregated lunch counters, I had a chance to find out.

Within weeks, we had organized students from Atlanta's black colleges in sit-in demonstrations at several downtown restaurants that would not serve black people. Seventy-seven of us were arrested, and I spent my first day in jail.

My next five years were spent in the movement—in voter registration drives in small towns across the South, on picket lines, at the March on Washington in 1963, and in Selma, Alabama, where the movement fought and won the right to vote in 1965.

By prompting the enactment of laws to protect all of us and by showing other Americans how to protest peacefully for their rights, the movement left America a different and a better place than it was before the movement began.

The history of that movement is told here through the stories of those who lost their lives. Some were killed because of their involvement in a demonstration or a registration drive. A few of them are well known; most are not. Some were killed—like Emmett Till—because they were black. Others—like Viola Liuzzo—died because they were white. Some—like Martin Luther King, Jr.—died because they dared to speak out for equality. Some—like four little girls in Sunday school—were simply easy targets of hate, in the wrong place at the wrong time.

When I look back on those years I wonder that a group of people as different as we were from each other could have been so successful in defeating a system of legalized white supremacy that had been in place for more than 100 years.

And when I look around me today, I realize that in spite of the victories that were won, much more remains to be done.

The civil rights movement of yesterday showed me, and millions of others, what determined people can do. People around the world have studied the American civil rights movement and applied its lessons to their problems.

Dissident students in China studied the United States's civil rights movement before planning the democracy demonstration in Tiananmen Square in 1989. When the Berlin Wall came down, the crowds on both sides sang "We Shall Overcome," the anthem of the American civil rights movement.

Wherever people face difficult problems—in their neighborhoods or across the nation—they can look at what happened in the southern United States three decades ago and believe that they too will overcome.

—Julian Bond

Preface

In Montgomery, Alabama, in 1989, a memorial was built to commemorate the achievements of the civil rights era and to honor those who died during that struggle. A few of the victims were well known — Medgar Evers, Martin Luther King Jr. — but there were many whose names you could not find in the history books: John Earl Reese, Willie Edwards, Clarence Triggs.

Along with a history of the civil rights movement, the stories of those who died are told here. Their lives serve as examples of the many personal tragedies suffered for a movement that transformed America from a society in which blacks were routinely excluded from full citizenship into one that now recognizes, if it has not entirely realized, the equal rights of all citizens.

Although civil rights activity has been a potent force in American political life since the Abolitionists battled slavery and continues in many forms today, the civil rights movement which overturned segregation in the South during the 1950s and 1960s was a unique phenomenon — characterized by nonviolent resistance and fueled by an enormous groundswell of support from ordinary people who had never before been politically involved.

The actions of politicians and judges helped speed the transformation that occurred during those 14 years. But it was the courage of people like Wharlest Jackson who lost their lives in the struggle that made that transformation inevitable.

Some of these martyrs were not killed because of anything they personally did, but because they represented, by their color, the movement that was threatening the segregationists' way of life. Lemuel Penn, driving through Georgia on his way home from Army reserve training; Willie Brewster, a foundry worker driving home from work; Virgil Ware, a boy on a bicycle — all were killed by members of large Klan and neo-Nazi organizations whose members thought terrorizing blacks would halt civil rights efforts.

But terrorism did not break the movement. Time after time, inhuman acts of violence only strengthened the dedication of those whose lives were bound to the struggle. When Emmett Till and Mack Parker were lynched in Mississippi, when four girls died in a Birmingham church explosion, people all over the world paid attention to the movement that was changing America, and the national will for reform grew.

Those whose deaths spurred the movement on, those who were killed by organized white terrorists trying to "set an example," and those who were murdered for their own acts of courage — these are the heroes of the civil rights struggle who are profiled in the following pages.

But they are not the only victims of the era. There are countless others who can only be characterized as victims of random, senseless racism — racism so perverse it allowed whites to murder blacks for little or no reason:

• Clinton Melton, a Sumner, Mississippi, service station worker, was killed in 1955 by a white man who objected to the price of his gasoline.

• L.C. Baldwin, a 79-year-old minister, was leading a cow along a roadside in Huntsville, Alabama, in the spring of 1956 when a young white man threw a 10-pound stone from a passing car "as a prank," killing Baldwin.

• Maybelle Mahone, a 30-year-old mother of six, was shot and killed by a white man at her home in Zebulon, Georgia, in 1956 because she "sassed" him.

• Frank Morris, a 51-year-old shoe repairman and radio host, was fatally burned when white men bombed his shop in Ferriday, Louisiana, on December 10, 1964.

Similar acts of racist violence have victimized blacks throughout history, and they have not ended. In 1981, a black man was randomly selected and lynched by the Klan in Mobile, Alabama. In 1988, neo-Nazi Skinheads murdered an Ethiopian man in Portland, Oregon, simply because he was black.

The research for the Civil Rights Memorial was conducted over a one-year period and included detailed searches through newspapers, state archives, Library of Congress holdings, and papers of civil rights organizations, as well as numerous personal interviews and hundreds of letters soliciting information.

From time to time during that research, a glimpse of a story kept appearing, in various forms, of the death of an unidentified teen-age boy whose body was found in September 1964 in the Big Black River near Canton, Mississippi. Several books noted his death in passing because he was found wearing a Congress of Racial Equality T-shirt, and other documents listed his death as the last in a long summer of violence in Mississippi. But nothing else was known about him, and it seemed his name had been forgotten.

After months of reading documents, a researcher scanning microfilm at the Library of Congress found a memo that noted the discovery of a body — a 14-year-old boy, wearing a CORE T-shirt, found in the Big Black River. His name was Herbert Oarsby.

The full story of Herbert Oarsby's death, and of racist violence in the civil rights era, may never be known. There were many deaths never investigated, many killers never identified, and many victims whose names have been lost.

This book is dedicated to the memory of Herbert Oarsby and the unknown martyrs of the civil rights movement.

PART 1

Early Struggles

Through two centuries of slavery and 90 years of legalized segregation, black Americans risked their lives for the cause of freedom.

Imagine being unable to eat or sleep in most restaurants or hotels; being unable to sit where you wanted in a movie theater; having to sit in the back when you boarded a bus, even an empty one; being forced to attend an inferior school; and even being forbidden to drink from certain water fountains.

These were the facts of everyday life for all black people in the Southern part of the United States as recently as 1960. They were citizens of a country founded on the principle that all men are created equal. Yet, they were treated unequally and declared unequal by law.

In the middle 1950s, a movement of ordinary women and men arose to challenge this way of life. Using boycotts, marches, and other forms of protest, they ultimately forced the South to end its peculiar system of legalized segregation. They succeeded because, in a democracy, when the people speak, the government must listen.

Historians usually trace the modern civil rights movement from May 17, 1954, when the Supreme Court outlawed segregation in public schools, to April 4, 1968, when Dr. Martin Luther King Jr. was assassinated in Memphis. But just as the death of the movement's most famous leader did not mark the end of the struggle for racial equality, the story — and the struggle — began much earlier.

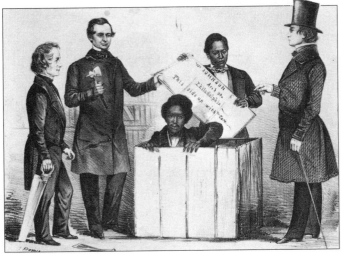

SLAVES IN THE NEW WORLD

The first settlers came to the New World seeking economic and religious freedom. In their yearning for power, however, they forced Native Americans from their land. Then in the early 1600s, the first Africans were brought to America and forced into a cruel system of slavery which was to flourish for 250 years.

As slavery grew, so did deep-seated feelings of racial superiority. Whites tried to

Left Above: The life of Africans in 17th century America began at the slave market, where they were sold to white masters.

Left Below: Henry Brown escaped his Virginia slave masters by hiding in a box bound for Philadelphia.

Above: Harriet Tubman helped more than 300 slaves escape from the South on the Underground Railroad.

justify owning their fellow men and women by claiming that blacks were less than human, unfit for civilization.

Legalized brutality kept slaves in their place. Slaves who revolted or tried to escape were beaten or hanged. It was against the law in many states to teach a slave to read or write. Anyone caught helping a runaway slave could be sent to prison.

Yet many people risked death in their yearning for freedom. A freed black man named Daniel Payne established a clandestine school for slaves in South Carolina. Teenage slave Ann Wood turned back an armed white posse with her shotgun and led a group of escaped slaves to freedom in Maryland. Former slave Harriet Tubman secretly guided 300 slaves out of the South on the "Underground Railroad."

Frederick Douglass fought off a cruel master and fled to freedom when he was a teenager. He taught himself to read and write and became the

SOJOURNER TRUTH

UNION SOLDIER

leading spokesman for the Abolitionist movement. Another former slave, Sojourner Truth, routinely defied segregation laws by refusing to leave white sections of trains and streetcars.

In demonstrating a willingness to risk everything for freedom, these early civil rights activists set an example that would inspire others a full century later. Their heroism also awakened many white Americans to the inhumanity of slavery. Northern whites in the Abolitionist movement provided shelter for escaping slaves and helped elect a president who would free the slaves.

After President Lincoln signed the Emancipation Proclamation in 1863, more than 200,000 Southern blacks left their masters to fight alongside Union troops in the Civil War. Former slaves also served as Union spies, ship pilots, and nurses. Twenty of them won the country's highest military award, the Medal of Honor.

BROKEN PROMISES

The end of the Civil War brought a brief glimpse of freedom. The Thirteenth Constitutional Amendment outlawed slavery; the Fourteenth Amendment protected the rights of the newly freed slaves; and the Fifteenth Amendment gave black citizens the right to vote.

In many Southern states blacks were elected to high offices, and black legislators helped write new state constitutions. Fourteen blacks served in the U.S. House of Representatives between 1870 and 1876. It seemed for a short time as if American society would live up to its founding principles.

But the promise of democracy was once again broken. Most Southern whites were determined to keep blacks poor, uneducated, and powerless. White reactionary politicians used corruption and force to re-establish their power in the South, and they met little opposition from the federal government. The reforms of Reconstruction began to erode.

The Ku Klux Klan, formed by a group of Confederate Army veterans, used terrorism and violence to re-establish the reign of white supremacy.

Between 1882 and 1901, nearly 2,000 blacks were lynched. One of the most widely publicized atrocities was the killing in April 1899 of Sam Hose, a black man accused of murder in Georgia. Hose was publicly mutilated then burned alive while a crowd of 2,000 cheered. Special trains were scheduled so whites from across the state could come to the lynching.

By 1910, blacks were caught in a degrading system of total segregation throughout the South. Through "Jim Crow" laws (named after a black minstrel in a popular song), blacks were ordered to use separate restrooms, water fountains, restaurants, waiting rooms, swimming pools, libraries, and bus seats.

The United States Supreme Court gave its approval to Jim Crow segregation in the 1896 case of *Plessy v. Ferguson*. The Court said separate facilities were legal as long as they were equal. In practice, Southern states never provided equal facilities to black

people — only separate ones.

Frederick Douglass tried to expose the inherent contradictions in the law of the land: "So far as the colored people of the country are concerned," he said, "the Constitution is but a stupendous sham…fair without and foul within, keeping the promise to the eye and breaking it to the heart."

Despite Douglass' eloquent arguments, it would be generations before the nation lived up to its promises.

FIGHTING JIM CROW

Just as slaves had revolted against being someone else's property, the newly freed blacks revolted peacefully against the forces of racism. Ida B. Wells began a crusade against lynching at age 19 that inspired a national gathering of black leaders in 1893 to call for an anti-lynch law.

George Henry White, the only black U.S. congressman at the turn of the century, was a bold spokesman for equal rights. The former slave from North Carolina sponsored the first anti-lynching bill and insisted that the federal government enforce the constitutional amendments. In a speech to his fellow congressmen, White asked, "How long will you sit in your seats and hear and see the principles that underlie the foundations of this government sapped away little by little?"

One of the strongest critiques of American racism was offered by W.E.B. DuBois, a Harvard-educated sociologist. In *The Souls of Black Folk,*

DuBois said American society had to be transformed if blacks were to achieve full equality.

DuBois, along with other black and white leaders, established the National Association for the Advancement of Colored People in 1910. The NAACP launched a legal campaign against racial injustice, began documenting racist violence, and published a magazine called *Crisis.* By 1940, NAACP membership reached 50,000.

As blacks were organizing for reform, white supremacists were organizing to stop them. By the time the NAACP was 10 years old, two million whites belonged to the Ku Klux Klan. During the 1920s, Klansmen

Opposite page. Former slave Frederick Douglass spoke boldly and eloquently in favor of equal rights for blacks.
Above. In the early 20th century, blacks marched in the streets of Washington, D.C., to show support for an anti-lynching bill. The bill was never passed.

held high positions in government throughout the country.

In the South, Klan violence surged. Blacks moved North in record numbers, hoping to escape racial terrorism and to find better jobs. Although they faced poverty, unequal education, and discrimination in the North as well, racial restrictions there were less harsh. Blacks could even vote in Northern states. Indeed, by 1944, the black vote was a significant factor in 16 states outside the South.

BRINGING DEMOCRACY HOME

With the election of President Franklin Delano Roosevelt, black Americans finally had an ally in the White House. Black leaders were included among the president's

Below. A black soldier who lost a leg in overseas combat during World War I views a parade of segregated U.S. Army troops in New York City in 1919.
Right. Signs designating "colored" facilities were commonplace throughout the South during the first half of the 20th century.

advisers. Roosevelt's New Deal made welfare and jobs available to blacks as well as whites. A more liberal Supreme Court issued rulings against bus segregation and all-white political primaries. Black labor leader A. Philip Randolph scored a major victory when he convinced President Roosevelt to issue an Executive Order banning racial discrimination in all defense industries.

The demand for equal rights surged after World War II, when black soldiers returned from battling the racist horrors of Nazi Germany only to find they remained victims of racism at home.

through the South and endured harassment without retaliating.

While the sit-ins and freedom rides of the 1940s served as models for the next generation of civil rights activists, they did not capture the broad support that was necessary to overturn segregation. The CORE victories were quiet ones, representing the determination of relatively few people.

The major battles against segregation were being fought in courtrooms and legislatures. Growing pressure from black leaders after World War II forced President Harry Truman to integrate the armed forces and to establish a civil rights commission. In 1947, that commission issued a report called *To Secure These Rights* that exposed racial injustices and called for the elimination of segregation in America.

By that time, half a million blacks belonged to the NAACP. Lawsuits brought by the NAACP had forced many school districts to improve black schools. Then, in 1950, NAACP lawyers began building the case that would force the Supreme Court to outlaw segregated schools and mark the beginning of the modern civil rights movement. ■

Determined to bring democracy to America, blacks sought new strategies. Seeing Mahatma Gandhi lead the Indian masses in peaceful demonstrations for independence, the Congress of Racial Equality decided to put the philosophy of nonviolence to work in America.

After much training and discussion, black and white members of CORE entered segregated restaurants, quietly sat down, and refused to leave until they were served. They did not raise their voices in anger or strike back if attacked. In a few Northern cities, their

persistent demonstrations succeeded in integrating some restaurants.

After the Supreme Court outlawed segregation on interstate buses in 1946, CORE members set out on a "Journey of Reconciliation" to test whether the laws were being obeyed. Blacks and whites rode together on buses

A Movement Of The People

Blacks in Montgomery and Little Rock faced down powerful white resistance to win the rights promised them by the Constitution.

Linda Brown's parents could not understand why their 7-year-old daughter should have to ride long distances each day to a rundown black school when there was a much better white school in their own neighborhood of Topeka, Kansas. Harry Briggs of Clarendon, South Carolina, was outraged that his five

children had to attend schools which operated on one-fourth the amount of money given to white schools. Ethel Belton took her complaints to the Delaware Board of Education when her children were forced to ride a bus for nearly two hours each day instead of

walking to their neighborhood high school in Claymont. In Farmville, Virginia, 16-year-old Barbara Johns led her fellow high school students on a strike for a better school.

All over the country, black students and parents were angered over the conditions of their schools. NAACP lawyers studied their grievances and decided that it was not enough to keep fighting for equal facilities. They wanted all schools integrated.

A team of NAACP lawyers used the Topeka, Clarendon, Claymont and Farmville examples to argue that segregation itself was unconstitutional. They lost in the lower courts, but when they took their cause to the Supreme Court, the justices ruled they were right.

On May 17, 1954, the Supreme Court unanimously ruled that segregated schools "are inherently unequal." The Court explained that even if separate schools for blacks and whites had the same physical facilities, there could be no true equality as long as segregation itself existed. To separate black children "solely because of their race," the Court wrote, "generates a feeling of inferiority as to their status in the community that may affect their hearts and minds in a way very unlikely ever to be undone."

The *Brown v. Board of Education* ruling enraged many Southern whites who did not believe blacks deserved the same education as whites and didn't want their children attending schools with black children. Southern governors announced they would not abide by the court's ruling, and White Citizens' Councils were organized to oppose school integration. Mississippi legislators passed a law abolishing compulsory school attendance. A declaration called the Southern Manifesto was issued by 96 Southern congressmen, demanding that the Court reverse the *Brown* decision.

Despite the opposition by many whites, the *Brown* decision gave great hope to blacks. Even when the Supreme Court refused to order immediate integration (calling instead for schools to act "with all deliberate speed"), black Americans knew that times were changing. And they were eager for expanded rights in other areas as well.

WALKING FOR JUSTICE

Four days after the Supreme Court handed down the *Brown* ruling, Jo Ann Robinson wrote a letter as president of the Women's Political Council to the mayor of Montgomery, Alabama. She represented a large group of black women, she said, and was asking for fair treatment on city buses.

Blacks, who made up 75 percent of Montgomery's bus riders, were forced to enter the buses in front, pay the driver, and re-enter the bus from the rear, where they could only sit in designated "colored" seats. If all the "white" seats were full, blacks had to give up their seats.

Women and children had been arrested for refusing to give up their seats. Others who challenged the bus drivers were slapped or beaten. Hilliard Brooks, 22, was shot dead by police in 1952 after an

Opposite page. The hopes of black Americans everywhere were hanging on the Supreme Court's decision in the *Brown v. Board of Education* case. Hours before the hearings began, people lined up to hear the arguments. Finally, on May 17, 1954, the Court ruled segregated schools were unconstitutional.
Below. Black protests against segregation, which had been voiced for centuries, were finally being heard in the mid-1950s.

Above. The Montgomery bus boycott succeeded because black women who depended on the buses for transportation refused to ride until they were granted fair seating. For more than a year, they took taxis, carpooled, walked and hitchhiked.

argument with a bus driver.

Every day, black housekeepers rode all the way home after work, jammed together in the aisles, while 10 rows of "white" seats remained empty.

Blacks could shut down the city's bus system if they wanted to, Jo Ann Robinson told the mayor. "More and more of our people are already arranging with neighbors and friends to ride to keep from being insulted and humiliated by bus drivers."

The mayor said segregation was the law and he could not change it.

On December 1, 1955, Rosa Parks was riding home from her job as a department store seamstress. The bus was full when a white man boarded. The driver stopped the bus and ordered Mrs. Parks along with three other blacks to vacate a row so the white man could sit down. Three of the blacks stood up. Rosa Parks

kept her seat and was arrested.

Jo Ann Robinson and the Women's Political Council immediately began to organize a bus boycott with the support of NAACP leader E.D. Nixon. Prominent blacks hurriedly formed the Montgomery Improvement Association and selected a newcomer in town, Dr. Martin Luther King Jr., to be their leader.

On the night of December 5, a crowd of 15,000 gathered at Holt Street Church to hear

Left. Montgomery blacks continued their boycott despite harassment and physical attacks by angry whites.
Below. Segregated bus seating forced blacks to sit in the back and give up their seats to white people on the orders of the driver.

the young preacher speak. "There comes a time that people get tired," King told the crowd. "We are here this evening to say to those who have mistreated us so long that we are tired — tired of being segregated and humiliated; tired of being kicked about by the brutal feet of oppression. …We have no alternative but to protest.

"And we are not wrong in what we are doing," he said.

"If we are wrong, the Supreme Court of this nation is wrong. If we are wrong, God Almighty is wrong!"

If the bus boycott was peaceful and guided by love, King said, justice would be won. Historians in future generations, King predicted, "Will have to pause and say, 'There lived a great people — a black people — who injected new meaning and dignity into the veins of civilization.' "

For 381 days, black people did not ride the buses in Montgomery. They organized car pools and walked long distances, remaining nonviolent even when harassed and beaten by angry whites. When Dr. King's home was bombed, they only became more determined. City officials tried to outlaw the boycott, but still the buses traveled empty.

On December 21, 1956, blacks returned to the buses in triumph. The U.S. Supreme Court had outlawed bus segregation in Montgomery in response to a lawsuit brought by the boycotters with the help of the NAACP. The boycotters' victory showed the entire white South that all blacks, not just civil rights leaders, were opposed to segregation. It demonstrated that poor and middle class blacks could unite to launch a successful protest movement, overcoming both official counterattacks and racist terror. And it showed the world that nonviolent resistance could work — even in Montgomery, the capital of the Confederate States during the Civil War.

King went on to establish an organization of black clergy, called the Southern Christian Leadership Conference, that raised funds for integration campaigns throughout the South. Black Southern ministers, following the example of King in Montgomery, became the spiritual force behind the nonviolent movement. Using the lessons of Montgomery, blacks challenged bus segregation in Tallahassee and Atlanta.

But when they tried to integrate schools and other public facilities, blacks discovered the lengths to which

whites would go to preserve white supremacy. A black student admitted to the University of Alabama by federal court

Above. Rosa Parks finally takes a seat in the front of the bus after the Supreme Court ruled bus segregation illegal.

Right. Governor George Wallace stood in the door of the University of Alabama to demonstrate his refusal to admit a black student to the school.

order was promptly expelled. The State of Virginia closed all public schools in Prince Edward County to avoid integration. Some communities filled in their public swimming pools and closed their tennis courts, and others removed library seats, rather than let blacks and whites share the facilities.

Blacks who challenged segregation received little help from the federal government. President Eisenhower had no enthusiasm for the *Brown* decision, and he desperately wanted to avoid segregation disputes.

Finally, in 1957, a crisis in Little Rock, Arkansas, forced Eisenhower to act.

NINE PIONEERS IN LITTLE ROCK

On September 4, 1957, Governor Orval Faubus ordered troops to surround Central High Shool in Little Rock, to keep nine black teenagers from entering. Despite the *Brown* ruling which said black students had a right to attend integrated schools,

Governor Faubus was determined to keep the schools segregated.

That afternoon, a federal judge ordered Faubus to let the black students attend the white school. The next day, when 15-year-old Elizabeth Eckford set out for class, she was mobbed, spit upon and cursed by angry whites. When she finally made her way to the front steps of Central High, National Guard soldiers turned her away.

An outraged federal judge again ordered the governor to let the children go to school. Faubus removed the troops but

gave the black children no protection. The nine black children made it to their first class, but had to be sent home when a violent white mob gathered outside the school. Faubus said the disturbance proved the school should not be integrated.

President Eisenhower had a choice: he could either send in federal troops to protect the children or allow a governor to defy the Constitution. Saying "our personal opinions have no bearing on the matter of enforcement," the president ordered in troops. For the rest of the school year, U.S. soldiers walked alongside the Little

Rock nine as they went from class to class.

The next year, Governor Faubus shut down all the public schools rather than integrate them. A year later, the U.S. Supreme Court ruled that "evasive schemes" could not be used to avoid integration, and the Little Rock schools were finally opened to black and white students.

Although the Little Rock case did not end the long battle for school integration, it proved the federal government would not tolerate brazen defiance of federal law by state officials. It also served as an

example for President John F. Kennedy who in 1962 ordered federal troops to protect James Meredith as he became the first black student to attend the University of Mississippi. ∎

Top. Elizabeth Eckford braved the angry white crowds by herself on the first day that nine black youths were admitted to Little Rock High.
Above. Many whites supported the official defiance of integration laws, and they elected politicians who voiced the strongest resistance to civil rights.

PART 3

By inviting confrontation but remaining nonviolent, civil rights activists demonstrated the justice of their cause and exposed the brutalities of racism.

Confront

One Monday afternoon in 1960, four black college students walked into a Woolworth's store in Greensboro, North Carolina. They bought a tube of toothpaste and some school supplies, then sat down at the lunch counter and ordered coffee. "We don't serve colored here," the waitress told them. The four young men kept their seats until the store closed.

The next day, they were joined by 19 other black students. By the week's end, 400 students, including a few whites, were sitting in shifts at the Woolworth's lunch counter. The following week, sit-ins were taking place in seven North Carolina cities.

No previous sit-in had captured the attention of young Americans like those in North Carolina. Youth in more

Black students in Nashville sat patiently at all-white lunch counters for hours, enduring harassment and violence and sometimes boredom in their determination to break down the walls of segregation.

ations

than 100 Southern cities conducted sit-ins against segregated restaurants, parks, swimming pools, libraries and theaters. Within a year, about 70,000 people had participated in sit-ins and 3,600 had been arrested. In some border states, young protesters succeeded in integrating lunch counters quietly and easily. But in the Deep South, they were beaten, kicked, sprayed with food, and burned with cigarettes. Many were arrested or expelled from school.

The sit-ins brought black youth into the front lines of the civil rights movement. Most of them were only children when the Supreme Court outlawed school segregation and they had grown into adulthood with the great hope that their rights would be fulfilled. When they saw how slow change was occurring, they became impatient with the established civil rights organizations. Seeking independence from the older generation, they formed a group called the Student Nonviolent Coordinating Committee (SNCC).

The young members of SNCC were heavily influenced by James Lawson, a Nashville theology student who had studied the nonviolent philosophy of Gandhi. Like Martin Luther King Jr., Lawson believed the power of Christian love could overcome the forces of hatred. Lawson taught students how to sit peacefully while being screamed at and spit upon, and how to fall into a position that protected their head and internal organs from beatings.

He told them it was honorable to go to jail for the cause of equality.

Even those who did not share the religious beliefs of Lawson and King saw the effectiveness of nonviolence. Over and over again, peaceful protesters were battered by fists and clubs simply for trying to exercise their rights. These spectacles of undeserved brutality tore at the consciences of most Americans and forced the federal government into action.

FREEDOM RIDES

On May 4, 1961, a group of blacks and whites set out on a highly publicized trip to test a Supreme Court order outlawing segregation in bus termi-

nals. Many of them belonged to the revitalized Congress of Racial Equality (CORE), which had tested integration laws during the 1940s. They called themselves Freedom Riders.

Ten days into their journey, on Mother's Day, the first bus of Freedom Riders pulled into the terminal at Anniston,

Alabama. Waiting for it was a mob of white men carrying pipes, clubs, bricks and knives. The bus driver quickly drove off, but the mob caught up with the bus again outside the city. They smashed the windows and tossed a firebomb into the bus. As the bus went up in flames, the riders rushed out into the hands of the mob and were brutally beaten.

When the second busload of Freedom Riders pulled into Anniston, eight white men boarded the bus and beat the occupants from the front to the rear. The most seriously injured was Walter Bergman, who was thrown to the floor and kicked unconscious. He suffered a stroke as a result of

arranged for the wounded Freedom Riders to fly out of Alabama, students in Nashville made plans to finish the Freedom Ride. Federal officials tried to discourage them, but the students were determined. They drove to Birmingham, but were arrested at the bus station and then driven back to the Alabama-Tennessee line, where they were left on a lonely highway late at night. They made their way back to

around the world. To avoid further bloodletting, the federal government had to act.

Having failed to stop the Freedom Riders, President Kennedy decided to protect them. Attorney General Robert Kennedy told Mississippi officials they could continue to enforce their segregation laws if they would guarantee the Freedom Riders' safety. From then on, the Freedom Riders traveled unharmed into Jackson,

Opposite page, above. Freedom Riders rest after being attacked by members of a white mob. The Riders were beaten and their bus was burned outside Anniston, Alabama.
Opposite page, below. John Lewis (left) and Jim Zwerg were wounded in the attack on Freedom Riders in Montgomery.
Left. Troops were finally brought in to protect the Freedom Riders after the series of attacks in Alabama. Many of the Riders were arrested and jailed in Jackson, Mississippi, at the end of their journey.

the beating and was confined to a wheelchair for life.

When the second group of Freedom Riders stepped off their bus in Birmingham, they were attacked by another white mob. Not a policeman was in sight to protect them. For ten minutes, the mob wildly beat the already-battered Freedom Riders. Several were hospitalized. Jim Peck, a long-time CORE activist, required 53 stitches to close his wounds.

As top federal officials

Birmingham and finally managed to get a bus to Montgomery. When their bus arrived in Montgomery, it was met by a mob of more than 1,000 whites who beat the Freedom Riders without police interference. This time, a presidential aide assigned to monitor the crisis was injured in the melee.

The unchecked mob violence was headline news

Mississippi, where they were promptly arrested and put in jail. By the end of the summer, 328 Freedom Riders had served time in Mississippi prisons.

Determined to put an end to the dangerous Freedom Rides, Attorney General Kennedy took the unusual step of asking the Interstate Commerce Commission to issue regulations against segregated terminals. In September, the Commission complied,

Luther King Jr., the Freedom Rides demonstrated "the real meaning of the movement: that students had faith in the future. That the movement was based on hope, that this movement had something within it that says somehow even though the arc of the moral universe is long, it bends toward justice."

King took that hope with him to Birmingham, Alabama, in 1963.

BIRMINGHAM

Birmingham was known as the South's most segregated city. The best schools and restaurants were closed to blacks. The better paying jobs in business and government were withheld from blacks. Terrorists had bombed 60 black homes and churches since the end of World War II, yet no one had been arrested. The city police were notorious for their brutality and racism.

When King came to Birmingham to lead anti-segregation boycotts and mass marches, Commissioner Eugene "Bull" Connor ordered his police officers to respond with force. Americans saw nightly news coverage of the Birmingham demonstrators being struck by police clubs, bitten by dogs, and knocked down by torrents of water strong enough to rip bark from trees.

Hundreds of demonstrators, including King, were arrested. While in jail, King responded to white ministers who urged him to be more patient in his demands. In his

ordering bus companies to obey the earlier Supreme Court ruling.

Once again, young protesters had exposed the injustices of segregation and forced the federal government to defend consitutional rights. Their courage also served to revive the student protest movement, which had slumped after the lunch counter sit-ins had ended. And they attracted fresh troops — many of them white and Northern — into the Southern civil rights movement.

Above all, said Martin

famous "Letter from a Birmingham Jail," King wrote, "I guess it is easy for those who have never felt the stinging darts of segregation to say, 'Wait.' " But, he said, "freedom is never voluntarily given by the oppressor; it must be demanded by the oppressed."

Many in the Birmingham movement were school children. For weeks, they begged to be allowed to march with the other civil rights demonstrators. Finally, on May 3, 1963, thousands of children — some as young as six years old — walked bravely through the police dogs and fire hoses and were arrested. Going to jail was their badge of honor.

The jailing of children horrified Americans, including Kennedy administration officials. Federal mediators were dispatched to Birmingham with orders to work out a settlement between King's forces and the city's business community. In the end, the businessmen agreed to integrate downtown facilities and to hire more blacks.

A DREAM SHARED

The victory in Birmingham fueled the movement,

Opposite page. Soaked from the fire hoses used by Birmingham police, civil rights activists struggled to contain their anger. Their protests remained nonviolent through continual attacks by police during the spring of 1963.
Above. Demonstrators huddled for protection under the force of water powerful enough to rip bark from the trees.
Left. Police used fierce attack dogs against the Birmingham civil rights marchers.

and civil rights activities spread throughout the United States. Even in the White House, the support for reform was growing.

On June 11, 1963, President Kennedy delivered his strongest civil rights message ever. "We face… a moral crisis," he said. "A great change is at hand, and our task, our obligation, is to make that revolution…peaceful and constructive for all." Only days later, Kennedy sent a comprehensive civil rights bill to Congress.

In August, a huge hopeful crowd of 250,000 blacks and whites marched on Washington to show support for the proposed bill. Martin Luther King Jr. addressed the crowd from the front of the Lincoln Memorial. The successes of 1963, he said, were "not an end, but a beginning.

"There will be neither rest nor tranquility in America until the Negro is granted his citizenship rights…We will not be satisfied until justice rolls down like waters and righteousness like a mighty stream."

The crowd cheered in jubilation as King's speech came to a close: "When we allow freedom to ring, when we let it ring from every village and every hamlet, from every state and city, we will be able to speed up that day when all of God's children — black men and white men, Jews and Gentiles, Catholics and Protestants — will be able to join hands and sing in the words of the old Negro spiritual, 'Free at last, free at last; thank God Almighty, we are free at last!' "

King's "I Have A Dream" speech would be remembered as a high point of the civil rights movement. Two weeks later, a dynamite explosion killed four Sunday School students at Birmingham's Sixteenth Street Baptist Church.

The Birmingham bombing and the assassination of President Kennedy two months

later created increased public support for a comprehensive civil rights law. The following summer, Congress passed the 1964 Civil Rights Act. By outlawing segregation in public accommodations, the new federal law validated the cause of the Freedom Rides and student sit-ins, and ensured the end of Birmingham-style segregation. But it did not address the problem of voting rights — that struggle was taking place on another bloody battleground. ■

Martin Luther King Jr. (in robe) prepares to speak to the massive crowd (right) that gathered in front of the Lincoln Memorial during the March on Washington.

PART 4

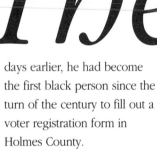

Fighting For The

Despite the elaborate restrictions designed to keep blacks from voting in the South, many risked their lives to vote. It was not until 1965, after a violent 'Freedom Summer' that black Southerners won full voting rights.

Less than a week after the children marched in Birmingham, two firebombs crashed into the Mississippi farmhouse of Hartman Turnbow. Before he could lead his wife and daughter out of the burning house, Turnbow had to fight off a gang of white men who were waiting outside.

The firebombing was Hartman Turnbow's punishment for trying to vote. A few days earlier, he had become the first black person since the turn of the century to fill out a voter registration form in Holmes County.

For blacks in the South, voting had always been dangerous business. Elaborate regulations limited black voting, and anyone who tried to defeat the system was punished. In 1958, for example, black farmer Izell Henry voted in a Democratic primary in Greensburg, Louisiana. The next morning, he was beaten by white men and left for dead. Henry lived, but suffered permanent brain damage.

Ballot

Attacks on black voters were common, but they were not the only tactics used to keep blacks away from the polls. State legislatures had more sophisticated tools. Until the mid-1960s, most Southern states had laws requiring voters to pay poll taxes, pass literacy tests, or read and interpret any section of the state constitution. Voter registrars applied the tests unequally. Blacks were rejected for mispronouncing a word while whites were approved who could not read at all.

At the whim of local officials, voting lists could be "purged" of unqualified voters. In four Louisiana parishes between 1961 and 1963, 90 percent of registered black voters were taken off the roles while only a handful of whites were removed.

Whites also used economic weapons against black voters. A voter registration worker in Southwest Georgia wrote in 1963 that "any [black person] who works for a white man in Terrell County and registers to vote can expect to lose his job." Others were denied loans

or had their rents doubled. To make the job of voter intimidation easier, Mississippi newspapers printed the names of all voter applicants.

One of the cruelest official actions against black voters was the food cut-off in LeFlore County, Mississippi, in the winter of 1962. In retaliation for an intense voter registration drive, county officials ended the government food surplus program that poor blacks depended on to get them through the winter. Voter registration workers organized a substitute relief program with nationwide support.

If terrorism, legal obstacles, and economic reprisals were not enough to stop black voter activity, there was also jail. Police arrested voter registration workers throughout the

Opposite page. An elderly man takes his turn at the voter registrar's table in Selma, Alabama. Until 1965, it was difficult and dangerous for blacks to vote in the South.
Above left. Voting rights demonstrators were attacked by state troopers at the Edmund Pettus Bridge in Selma, Alabama.
Above. Violence against Southern voting activists attracted the attention of Northern protesters.

South for charges such as distributing handbills without a license, inciting to riot, contributing to the delinquency of minors, and disturbing the peace.

When Hartman Turnbow's house was firebombed,

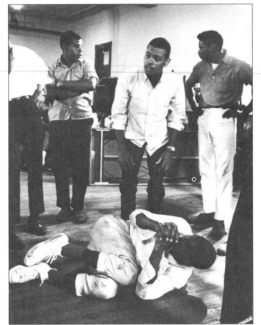

Amite County, he was arrested for interfering with an officer and spent three nights in jail. The second time, he was beaten. Moses' friend Herbert Lee was killed for helping in the voter registration drive.

Against such odds, Moses and others made slow progress in registering voters. And they had a long way to go. Although blacks made up nearly half the population in Mississippi, only five percent were registered to vote. In some counties, not a single black person was registered.

FREEDOM SUMMER

Black voting became a crucial goal of the civil rights movement. Civil rights activists knew that a few highly publicized integration campaigns

Turnbow and voter registration worker Bob Moses were arrested for arson. The sheriff said they set the fire themselves to draw sympathy for their voting rights campaign.

Bob Moses had been working for SNCC in Southwest Mississippi since 1961 and was no stranger to intimidation. The first time he accompanied black voter applicants to the courthouse in

Opposite page, left. Voter registration forms in Mississippi required applicants to interpret a section of the state constitution before they were allowed to vote.
Opposite page, right. Student volunteers for Freedom Summer were trained in techniques of nonviolence, including how to fall under the blows of an attacker.
Left. Preparing to leave for Mississippi, Northern college students join hands and sing.
Below. Veteran activist Bob Moses educates a group of students about the dangers they will face as civil rights volunteers in Mississippi.

would not sustain the movement. Only by building significant voting strength would Southern blacks be able to keep pressure on the government to protect their rights.

Several leading civil rights groups combined forces to establish the Council of Federated Organizations (COFO) voter registration project. COFO workers helped blacks fill out the complicated voter registration forms. They also helped poor people get government assistance and taught black children how to read and write.

As a result of COFO efforts, the number of black voters in the South rose steadily. But it was a long uphill battle against a harsh set of obstacles. Many blacks were afraid of reprisals or intimidat-

ed by the complicated requirements of registration. COFO activists became more and more frustrated. Instead of teaching blacks how to comply with unconstitutional laws, they wanted the laws changed altogether. Yet their demands for new federal legislation went unanswered.

In 1964, COFO launched a campaign called Freedom Summer to bring attention to the voting abuses. A thousand college students — most of them white — were brought to Mississippi to register voters and teach in Freedom Schools. Black voters had suffered years of repression, and the barriers to voting remained. If the white volunteers were beaten or arrested for voting activites, civil rights leaders reasoned,

the country might take notice.

No one anticipated the magnitude of the violence that would follow. On the first day of Freedom Summer, three workers — Michael Schwerner, Andrew Goodman, and James Chaney — were kidnapped and killed, and their bodies were buried deep in an earthen dam. By the end of the summer, 37 black churches had been burned, 30 homes bombed, 80 civil rights workers beaten, and more than 1,000 arrested.

The brutal white response to Freedom Summer brought national attention to racism in Mississippi and

Above. Sheriff Jim Clark's posse, armed with clubs, faced down the Selma marchers. The standoff lasted until a federal court permitted the march to go on.

Right. A Selma marcher comforts an injured companion after they were attacked by state troopers using tear gas and clubs.

strengthened support for voting rights legislation. People everywhere saw that black people in Mississippi were determined to win their rights, even if it meant risking their lives.

By August, 80,000 blacks in Mississippi had joined the Mississippi Freedom Democratic Party in a direct challenge to the state's segregationist Democratic party. Led by veteran activists Fannie Lou Hamer, Victoria Gray, Annie Divine, and Aaron Henry, 64 delegates from the Freedom Democratic Party attended the Democratic National Convention. Although it was not officially recognized, the delegation brought worldwide attention to the cause of voting rights in Mississippi.

THE SELMA MARCH

In Alabama, too, blacks had been demonstrating for voting rights. Since 1963, blacks in Marion and Selma had been marching to the courthouse to register, only to be turned back by police. Then in early 1965, Martin Luther King Jr. came to Selma, bringing with him the attention of national media. King's nightly mass meetings inspired more blacks to join the struggle, and the marches were stepped up. Hundreds were arrested.

Once again, it was the spectacle of senseless violence that caused the nation to respond. On February 26, 1965, Jimmy Lee Jackson was shot and killed by a state trooper in nearby Marion. On March 7, demonstrators

attempting to march from Selma to the state capitol in Montgomery were brutally beaten back by state troopers. Days later, Rev. James Reeb, a civil rights volunteer from Boston, was beaten to death on a Selma street.

King issued a nationwide appeal for support, and thousands came from all over the country to join in the march to

Above left. Children took their turn to march and go to jail during the long series of voting rights demonstrations in Selma during 1965.
Above right. A lone white woman voices her support for the Selma marchers.
Left. Martin Luther King Jr. walks beside SNCC representative James Forman (in overalls and tie) at the start of the Selma to Montgomery march.

Montgomery. On March 25 , after four days of walking, a huge crowd gathered at the state capitol.

King spoke to them about the importance of being able to vote. "The Civil Rights Act of 1964 gave Negroes some part of their rightful dignity, but without the vote it was dignity without strength.

"We are still in for a season of suffering," King warned them. But violence would not stop the movement. "We must keep going."

Later that day, Viola Gregg Liuzzo, a Michigan mother of five, was shot and killed by Klansmen as she was helping to transport Selma marchers. In response to the Selma march and the murders of Jackson, Reeb and Liuzzo, Congress passed the Voting Rights Act on July 9, 1965. The bill outlawed obstacles to black voting and authorized federal officials to enforce fair voting practices. All over the South, thousands of blacks were registered to vote the next year. ■

Days Of Rage

The civil rights movement ended legal apartheid in the South and forever changed relations between blacks and whites. It continues today in the battle against inequalities and injustices that remain.

By 1965, the civil rights movement had won broad new legislation protecting the rights of black citizens. After the passage of the 1964 Civil Rights Act and the 1965 Voting Rights Act, the federal government took a much greater role in monitoring school integration, registering black voters, and prosecuting racially motivated crimes.

The movement gave black people throughout America a renewed pride. They had

forced a federal government to recognize its responsibilities. They had established their own political strength. They had seen the rise of new and powerful black leaders. They had witnessed the structures of segregation dismantled by the courageous acts of ordinary people like themselves.

Yet the exhilarating successes of the movement were accompanied by tensions within its ranks. Some of the younger civil rights activists criticized Martin Luther King Jr.

for devoting resources to mass marches instead of grassroots political organizing. Some questioned the doctrine of nonviolence. Others objected to the role played by whites in the movement and said blacks should build their own independent political structures.

The Vietnam War raised another point of contention — some civil rights activists argued that the war drained national resources from the struggle against poverty and injustice at home; others

thought civil rights and foreign policy should remain separate.

The more militant activists became increasingly frustrated with the slow pace of change and the politics of the more conservative leaders. The students in SNCC asked whites to leave their organization and chose black militant Stokely Carmichael as their leader. They took up the phrase "black power" to describe their new focus on building black-led political organizations in the South.

Malcolm X gained popularity as a nationwide spokesman for black power. A Black Muslim, Malcolm criticized the strategy of nonviolence, saying "it is criminal to teach a man not to defend himself when he is the constant victim of brutal attacks." (Malcom renounced violence and urged blacks not to hate whites shortly before his assassination on February 21, 1965.)

The message of black militancy struck a chord in many urban youth whose lives were not affected by the successes of the civil rights movement. They lived in the midst of crime and poverty, they attended inadequate schools and dropped out early, and they had little chance to get decent jobs. New civil rights laws could not change the fact that their own futures were dim.

Frustrated by a movement that seemed to be passing them by, many young blacks took their fury to the streets.

Cities erupted all across

Opposite page. Violence erupted during a protest in Memphis, a week before Martin Luther King Jr. was assassinated there.
Above. Two young girls run from police during the second day of rioting in New York City.

America during four consecutive summers. In 1964, black areas of New York City, Chicago and Philadelphia were torn by rioting. The next summer, the worst riot in decades destroyed the Watts section of Los Angeles — leaving 34 people dead, 5,000 under arrest, and millions of dollars of property burned. The rioting continued through the summer of 1967. By the time it was over, more than 17,000 people had

moving toward two societies, one black and one white — separate and unequal."

NEW DIRECTIONS

The riots dismayed civil rights activists, both militant and conservative, and awakened them to the enormous problems faced by urban blacks — problems that called for something more than sit-ins and mass marches.

Seeking a new direction

Poor People's March to go to Memphis, where striking sanitation workers had asked for his support. There, he was shot and killed by James Earl Ray on the balcony of the Lorraine Motel on April 4, 1968.

King's dream of a movement rejuvenated by poor people never came true. Black anger erupted again after his assassination, and many cities imposed curfews to halt further outbreaks of violence.

By that time, the weight of public opinion had turned against the militant factions in the movement. The federal government, through the FBI, began a campaign to destroy groups like CORE and SNCC by using illegal wiretaps and informers and by spreading false information about them.

Their movement divided by philosophy and by sabotage, traditional civil rights leadership took up the task of crisis management. They worked to ease tensions in the ghettos and maintain calm during tense school desegregation battles. At the same time they began to address the complex racial problems that remained — including inequalities in housing, education, job opportunities, and health care. Those inequalities are still the concerns of civil rights activists today.

been arrested, nearly 100 were dead, and over 4,000 were injured.

That summer, President Johnson appointed a special commission to study the causes of urban race rioting. On March 2, 1968, the Kerner Commission released its report, and warned that America "is

for the movement and an alternative to violence, Martin Luther King Jr. planned a Poor People's March on Washington for 1968. He hoped to revitalize the movement by bringing together all poor people — black and white.

In March 1968, King took a break from planning the

THE CIVIL RIGHTS LEGACY

From Montgomery to Memphis, the civil rights movement won great changes in American life. It ended legal apartheid in the American

whelming that blacks and whites do not have equal chances in America.

While the most degrading structures of discrimination were brought down, many of the attitudes that supported those structures still exist. Those attitudes are seen in the hundreds of cross burnings, vandalisms, and attacks that victimize minorities each year. They are advertised by the thousands of young neo-Nazi Skinheads who listen to racist rock music, brand themselves with swastikas, and boast about 'bashing' minorites. And they are seen daily in racial slurs scrawled on school lockers or shouted at the football games, racist jokes told among friends, and voluntary segregation in school cafeterias.

As long as inequalities and racial prejudice remain, the work of the civil rights movement — *our* work — will not be finished. But we know it can be accomplished, because the civil rights movement of the past has proved that ordinary people can change their world. The victories of the movement were won by a largely anonymous mass of citizens, black and white, many of them young, who dared to risk life and limb for freedom's cause. And they were won because the strength of our democratic form of government is its ability to respond to the people. That is why, as long as we have injustice — and people willing to make it their cause — the movement will continue on. ▪

Opposite page. A North Carolina woman carries homemade sign in protest.
Above left. Civil rights activists launched a mass march in an all-white Georgia county in January of 1987 — a week after an earlier march was attacked by Klansmen.
Below left. Demonstrators wave American flags at the Alabama State Capitol.

South and forever changed relations between blacks and whites. It emboldened black and other non-white Americans. In the process, it gave new life to the movement for women's rights and to the yearnings of other disadvantaged groups.

But two decades of progress could not erase centuries of oppression. Statistics show that more than thirty years after the Montgomery bus boycott, blacks in America are still more likely than whites to die in infancy, live in poverty, and drop out of school. Blacks earn less money than whites and work at lower skilled jobs. Most live in segregated neighborhoods, and many still attend schools that are poorer and predominantly black. The evidence is over-

Rev. George Lee
1903 -1955

"Rev. Lee did not just tell the people what they ought to do. He gave them an example ... He fought for equality and first class citizenship and he asked them to follow him."

– Roy Wilkins,
NAACP Executive Director.

In 1954, blacks in Belzoni, Mississippi outnumbered whites two to one. But like all Southern blacks, they were not allowed to attend white schools. They were forbidden to eat in white restaurants. They would be arrested if they sat in bus seats reserved for whites. And they did not vote.

Integration would be a long time coming to the small Delta town on the banks of the Yazoo River. Rev. George Lee, a black minister who also ran a local grocery store and printing press, had no illusions that it would come in his lifetime or that it would come without a struggle.

But Lee knew where the change would have to begin: at the ballot box. Despite the Supreme Court's recent ruling that outlawed school segregation, Lee knew there would be no equality for blacks in Belzoni until they could vote.

FULL-FLEDGED CITIZENSHIP

George Lee was born and raised in poverty on a Mississippi plantation. His only education came from the segregated plantation school. By the time he came to Belzoni, he possessed two valuable skills — typesetting and preaching — and he planned to use both to help blacks improve their lives.

When he began preaching about voting at black Baptist churches in and around Belzoni in the early 1950s, it was as if he were advocating revolution. Not only were there no black voters in Humphreys County, but "they weren't even thinking about it," said Rosebud Lee Henson, Lee's widow.

It would be another 10 years before civil rights workers launched a massive campaign to win voting rights in Mississippi. Throughout the 1960s, they would suffer beatings and arrests. For a black man to raise his voice against discrimination in 1954 was an unimaginable risk. Lee knew that.

With the help of his friend Gus Courts, Lee started a chapter of the National Association for the Advancement of Colored People (NAACP). They printed leaflets and held meetings, urging blacks to pay the poll tax (a fee for voting that was later ruled illegal) and to register to vote.

Whites in town immediately organized a White Citizens Council to fight back. The names of blacks registered to vote were put on a list and circulated to white businessmen who retaliated by firing them from their jobs, denying them credit and raising their rent.

In the face of white resistance, George Lee was a clever diplomat. At a meeting of county officials, Lee thanked the white leadership for its "generosity," and then gently suggested: "Whereas all the bordering counties are permitting Negroes to pay poll taxes, register and vote without any ill effects, we feel sure that the same could happen in this county....We respectfully ask that you will at this time endorse and support our efforts to become full-fledged citizens in this county."

COULDN'T BE BOUGHT

The white men who ran Belzoni were not interested in giving the power of the ballot to a black population which outnumbered them and could easily out-vote them. They decided George Lee had to be stopped.

One day a few of the white leaders came to visit Lee, and told him they had decided to let him and his wife vote as long as he stopped trying to get other blacks to vote. "George told them he appreciated that," his widow remembered, "but he wanted everyone to have a chance. And then they knew that he couldn't be bought."

Within a year, Lee and Courts convinced 92 black people to register. Then the white resistance turned violent. Blacks found their car windshields busted out. A black club was ransacked, and a note was left behind reading, "This is what will happen to Negroes who try to vote."

Lee and Courts regularly received death threats. Lee tried to take precautions, but he knew his days were numbered. Rose begged him to slow down his activities. But, she remembered, "He said somebody had to lead."

On the Saturday before Mother's Day in 1955, Lee was driving toward home when he was hit by gunfire from a passing car. With half his face blown apart, Lee pulled himself out of the car and made his way to a cab stand. Two black drivers took him to the hospital where he died.

HE GAVE THEM AN EXAMPLE

Without conducting an investigation, the sheriff concluded that Lee was fatally

1955

It took great courage for a black person to register to vote in Mississippi in the 1950s. Many, like George Lee, were willing to risk their jobs, their homes and their own lives in order to exercise their constitutional right.

injured in a traffic accident. When doctors pointed out the lead pellets taken from Lee's head and face, the sheriff said they were probably dental fillings. Even after he was informed that dentists didn't use lead for fillings, the sheriff refused to investigate. In the end, a coroner's jury ignored the evidence that Lee was murdered and ruled that he died of unknown causes.

NAACP officials called Lee's murder the most brutal act in a campaign of terrorism against black people who tried to vote. A celebration of the first anniversary of the *Brown v. Board* decision was turned into a memorial service for Lee. NAACP Executive Director Roy Wilkins addressed the capacity crowd:

"Rev. Lee did not just tell the people what they ought to do. He gave them an example: he did these things himself. He fought for equality and first class citizenship and he asked them to follow him."

Wilkins urged blacks to continue the struggle that Lee began in Belzoni. Many were so terrified by Lee's murder that they removed their names from the voter rolls, but Gus Courts was determined not to back down. Then, six months after Lee's death, Courts was hit by shots from a passing car. He recovered from his injuries but his assailants were never caught. Finally, yielding to the fears of his family, Courts abandoned his voter registration efforts and moved to Chicago. ■

Lamar Smith
1892 -1955

Lamar Smith, a 63-year-old World War II veteran, commanded unusual wealth and respect for a black Mississippian in the 1950s. He ran a profitable farm, belonged to several prestigious black lodges, and enjoyed fishing and hunting with whites as well as blacks.

Nevertheless, Smith was shot dead by a white man in broad daylight, while a crowd of people watched. And no one was ever tried for his murder because not a single eyewitness would testify that they saw a white man kill a black man.

Lamar Smith's murder remains largely a mystery. But there is little doubt that it had to do with politics.

FEARLESS CAMPAIGNER

At a time when Mississippi law and white threats kept most blacks from voting, Lamar Smith was determined that his people would have a say in local government. He fearlessly organized black voters in Lin-coln County, campaigned for candidates he judged to be fair, and even helped organize absentee-ballot drives among blacks. (It was common practice among whites in the county to misuse absentee ballots.)

Blacks still only made up a small percentage of the total vote, but with Lamar Smith's efforts, their strength was growing. They might not be able to elect a black candidate, but they could at least make the white politicians pay attention to them.

Lamar Smith was one man who was not afraid to make his voice heard. In July 1955, he campaigned hard against an incumbent county supervisor. He cast his own vote in the August 2nd primary election, and was spending the final days before the run-off election campaigning among black voters.

On Saturday, August 13 — nine days before the run-off — Smith went down to

At a time when Mississippi law and white threats kept most blacks from voting, Lamar Smith was determined that his people would have a say in local government.

the county courthouse on business. As he stood on the lawn, he was approached by several white men who began arguing with him. The courthouse lawn was a popular weekend gathering place, and a number of people watched as one of the white men pulled out a .38-caliber pistol and shot Lamar Smith at close range.

Brookhaven Sheriff Robert Case was close enough to hear the gunshot and see a blood-splattered white man leave the scene. But it was eight days before he arrested three men for the murder.

SILENT WITNESSES

Although many people had witnessed the argument and the shooting, no one was willing to testify to what they saw on the courthouse lawn that Saturday. Without evidence, the grand jury could return no indictments, and the three white men went free.

The grand jury's report noted that "although it was generally known or alleged to be known who the parties were in the shooting, yet people standing within 20 or 30 feet at the time claim to know nothing about it, and most assuredly

somebody has done a good job of trying to cover up the evidence in this case…."

No evidence has survived to shed light on why Lamar Smith was killed. Prosecutor E.C. Barlow characterized the murder as political, rather than racial. It was "the direct result of local disputes, local politics in the race for Supervisor…."

An NAACP investigation showed that Lamar Smith "had received several threats on his life if he did not slow down on his political activities." NAACP Special Counsel Thurgood Marshall (who 12 years later became the nation's first black Supreme Court justice) wrote that Smith's murder was part of ongoing black voter intimidation in Mississippi and noted that Smith was killed three months after voter registration organizer George Lee was murdered in Belzoni.

One white man who had known Smith for nearly 15 years and considered himself a friend said Lamar Smith was killed for one simple reason: he refused to accept second-class citizenship as a black man. "I'm sure if there was any reason for the shooting it was that Smith thought he was as good as any white man." ■

In rural areas where blacks made up a large percentage of the population, whites in power went to extremes to prevent them from voting. Leaders like Lamar Smith helped blacks file absentee ballots so they wouldn't have to risk going to the polls to vote. When blacks in the South finally won the ballot in the mid-1960s, their votes became a significant factor in all elections.

Emmett Louis Till
1941-1955

"The fact that Emmett Till, a young black man, could be found floating down the river in Mississippi just set in concrete the determination of the people to move forward."

– Fred Shuttlesworth

Mamie Till was a devoted, well-educated mother who taught her son that a person's worth did not depend on the color of his or her skin. Nevertheless, when she put 14-year-old Emmett on a train bound for Mississippi in the summer of 1955, she warned him: "If you have to get down on your knees and bow when a white person goes past, do it willingly."

It was not in Emmett Till to bow down. Raised in a working-class section of Chicago, he was bold and self-assured. He didn't understand the timid attitude of his Southern cousins toward whites. He even tried to impress them by showing them a photo of some white Chicago youths, claiming the girl in the picture was his girlfriend.

One day he took the photo out of his wallet and showed it to a group of boys standing outside a country store in Money, Mississippi. The boys dared him to speak to a white woman in the store. Emmett walked in confidently, bought some candy from Carolyn Bryant, the wife of the store owner, and said "Bye baby" on his way out.

Within hours, nearly everyone in town had heard at least one version of the incident. Some said Emmett had asked Mrs. Bryant for a date; others said he whistled at her. Whatever the details were, Roy Bryant was outraged that a black youth had been disrespectful to his wife. That weekend, Bryant and his half-brother J.W. Milam went looking for Till. They came to the cotton field shack that belonged to Mose Wright, a 64-year-old farmer and grandfather of Emmett Till's cousin. Bryant demanded to see "the boy that did the talking." Wright reluctantly got Till out of bed. As the white men took Emmett Till away, they told Wright not to cause any trouble or he'd "never live to be 65."

A magazine writer later paid Milam to describe what happened that night. Milam said he and Bryant beat Emmett

Till, shot him in the head, wired a 75-pound cotton gin fan to his neck and dumped his body in the Tallahatchie River.

When asked why he did it, Milam responded: "Well, what else could I do? He thought he was as good as any white man."

SO THE WORLD COULD SEE

Till's body was found three days later — a bullet in the skull, one eye gouged

out and the head crushed in on one side. The face was unrecognizable. Mose Wright knew it was Till only because of a signet ring that remained on one finger. The ring had belonged to Emmett's father Louis, who had died ten years earlier, and bore his initials L.T.

Mamie Till demanded the body of her

son be sent back to Chicago. Then she ordered an open-casket funeral so the world could see what had been done to Emmett. *Jet* magazine published a picture of the horribly disfigured corpse. Thousands viewed the body and attended the funeral.

All over the country, blacks and sympathetic whites were horrified by the killing. Thousands of people sent money to the NAACP to support its legal efforts on behalf of black victims.

In the meantime, J.W. Milam and Roy Bryant faced murder charges. They admitted they kidnapped and beat Emmett Till, but claimed they left him alive. Ignoring nationwide criticism, white Mississippians raised $10,000 to pay the legal expenses

for Milam and Bryant. Five white local lawyers volunteered to represent them at the murder trial.

Mose Wright risked his life to testify against the men. In a courtroom filled with reporters and white spectators, the frail black farmer stood and identified Bryant and Milam as the men who took Emmett away.

Wright's act of courage didn't convince the all-white jury. After deliberating just over an hour, the jury returned a verdict of not guilty.

The murder of Emmett Till was the spark that set the civil rights movement on fire. For those who would become leaders of that movement, the martyred 14-year-old was a symbol of the struggle for equality.

"The Emmett Till case shook the foundations of Mississippi," said Myrlie Evers, widow of civil rights leader Medgar Evers. "…because it said even a child was not safe from racism and bigotry and death."

NAACP Executive Director Roy Wilkins said white Mississippians "had to prove they were superior…by taking away a 14-year-old boy."

Fred Shuttlesworth, who eight years later would lead the fight for integration in Birmingham, said, "The fact that Emmett Till, a young black man, could be found floating down the river in Mississippi just set in concrete the determination of the people to move forward…only God can know how many Negroes have come up missing, dead and killed under this system with which we live." ■

Left. The all-white jury listened to the evidence against Emmett Till's murderers, then took little more than an hour to find them not guilty.
Above. Mamie Till was overcome with grief when the body of her son arrived at the Chicago train station.

John Earl Reese
(photo unavailable)
1939-1955

Near midnight in a small cafe, John Reese and his cousin, Joyce Faye Nelson, were dancing to a song on the radio and drinking sodas. There was little else for black teen-agers to do on Saturday night in the tiny East Texas town of Mayflower.

This night, the party at the Mayflower cafe was shattered by a sudden burst of gunfire. Nine bullets crashed through the walls and windows of the cafe. The force of one bullet slammed John to the floor. He grabbed instinctively for his cousin, then fell dead. A second bullet struck Joyce Nelson in the arm, and a third wounded her sister sitting in a nearby booth.

The gunmen drove quickly past the cafe and on to other targets. They shot into a black school and a school bus. Their gunfire barely missed a black woman kneeling by her bedside praying. By the time it was all over, 27 bullets had ripped through the community of Mayflower, leaving its black citizens terrified and a 16-year-old boy dead.

SCARE TACTICS

It wasn't the first night of terror in Mayflower. In the months since voters had approved funds for a new black school, angry whites had repeatedly driven through town, firing into black homes and vehicles. "They're trying to scare the Negroes out of their citizenship," said the white school superintendent.

For years, blacks throughout the country had fought for better school conditions

for their children, under the "separate but equal" doctrine. Then the Supreme Court in 1954 recognized that "separate" black schools were never "equal" to white schools, and ordered all public schools integrated. But whites throughout the South were determined to keep their schools segregated, even if that meant breaking the law.

Blacks in Mayflower knew that full integration was still impossible, so they continued their struggle for improved segregated facilities in the face of white violence.

It was common knowledge that white men from Tatum were responsible for the nighttime shooting sprees in Mayflower. After the first raid, however, police protected the whites from prosecution by arresting two black men for the shootings. The suspects, afraid of being jailed or beaten, pleaded guilty and were fined $15. The investigation was closed.

Even after the second raid and the murder of Reese, prosecutors continued to ignore the pattern of harassment. The

police failed to do tests on any of the bullet slugs and refused to interview the man most suspected of firing the shots: a 22-year-old rowdy named Dean Ross.

A PERSISTENT EDITOR

One man refused to let the story die. Ronnie Dugger, the white editor of *The Texas Observer* newspaper in Austin, drove to Mayflower, located bullet slugs, interviewed Dean Ross and talked to blacks who had been terrorized by the shootings.

Dugger wrote a series of stories detailing the crimes and criticizing the official investigation. His articles attracted the attention of Washington journalist Sarah McClendon, who wrote in her nationally syndicated column that Mayflower "now has a record far surpassing the Till murder in Mississippi."

Although people like Dugger and McClendon wanted the U.S. Justice Department to take over the investigation, officials in Washington declined.

Dugger did not give up.

In an editorial headlined "Justice Would be a Miracle," Dugger wrote:

"It is a hideous and sub-human crime that has been committed….What happened before Oct. 22 —the shootings that were not stopped — is a disgrace to the civilized conscience. What happened Oct. 22 — the murder and wounding of innocents — seems but another consequence of the nurture of prejudice in the incubus of community. But what has happened since Oct. 22 — the initial suppression by the press, the insupportable denials of the most obvious motive theory, the spectacle of the Attorney General willing to mouth these denials without making his own inquiry — these things are a blot on the honor of this free state."

Officials tried to silence Dugger by accusing him of interfering with the investigation, but they could not ignore the information he published.

'IRRESPONSIBLE BOYS'

After three months, police arrested Dean Ross and Joe Simpson for the murder of John Reese. In announcing the arrests, the prosecutor characterized Reese's murder as "a case of two irresponsible boys attempting to have some fun by scaring Negroes."

Dean Ross admitted to the earlier raids for which the two black men had been charged and he gave detailed descriptions of the October 22 shootings as well. He was convicted of murder, but received only a brief suspended sentence and served no time. The prosecutor dismissed the case against Joe Simpson.

The official disregard for justice in the murder of John Reese disturbed both whites and blacks in Texas. One white man, a Methodist minister, wrote in *The Texas Observer* that John Reese was a victim of a racist society.

There is "a general lack of regard for Negroes in East Texas," wrote Rev. Guston H. Browning. "A Negro is considered by many as something just a little less than human…Whether or not a direct connection between this murder and the conflict over the Negro school can be positively established, I do not know. But that a shameful, non-Christian feeling of racial superiority is at the base of it all, I would bet my life…." ■

Under the "separate but equal" doctrine, black schools were allowed to deteriorate while white schools received the bulk of school funds. Blacks in rural areas had to fight for improvements in their schools even after the Supreme Court ruled school segregation unconstitutional.

Willie Edwards Jr.
1932 -1957

"Jump," they said. Edwards saw his only chance of survival in the dark Alabama River below him, and he jumped.

Every victory of the civil rights struggle brought a backlash of brutality. When blacks in Montgomery finally won the right to fair seating on city buses in December 1956, they were harassed and beaten by angry whites. Klansmen marched in robes through the city streets to intimidate black bus riders. A white gang attacked a teen-age girl as she got off the bus. And a pregnant woman was shot in the leg by white snipers.

Then, early one Sunday morning, dynamite bombs ripped through four churches and several homes belonging to ministers sympathetic to the bus boycotters. Two Klansmen — Sonny Kyle Livingston and Raymond York — were arrested. Martin Luther King Jr. was among the spectators who packed the courtroom when they went to trial.

King wrote later: "The defense attorneys spent two days...arguing that the bombings had been carried out by the MIA (the Montgomery Improvement Association, which sponsored the boycott) in order to inspire new outside donations for their dwindling treasury...On the other hand (the prosecutor) had an excellent case. The men had signed confessions. But in spite of all the evidence, the jury returned a verdict of not guilty...Raymond D. York and Sonny Kyle Livingston walked grinning out of the courtroom."

Years later, in a dramatic confession to authorities, a Klansman described a murder which had taken place in the aftermath of the Montgomery bus boycott. Since the bombings had left no victims, he said, several Klan members decided to kill a black man. They picked a black truck driver who they suspected was dating a white woman. Instead, they killed Willie Edwards Jr. by mistake.

MISTAKEN IDENTITY

On January 23, Edwards came home tired from his job as a truck driver for Winn Dixie supermarkets. Less than an hour after he got home, a supervisor telephoned and asked him to come back to work. Another driver had called in sick, and Edwards was needed to drive his route.

Willie Edwards had begun driving a delivery route for Winn Dixie in 1953 — a year before the Supreme Court outlawed school segregation and two years before Rosa Parks was arrested in Montgomery for refusing to give up her seat on a bus. He and his wife Sarah Jean and their three young children lived in Montgomery but kept their distance from the dangerous business of civil rights. Edwards had never participated in the boycott and he had few ambitions beyond providing for his family and contributing to the work of his church.

The night Willie Edwards was called in to substitute for his co-worker, a carload of Klansmen was waiting near the Montgomery County line for a black driver in a Winn Dixie truck who they heard was dating a white woman. When Edwards appeared, they stopped him and ordered him to get in their car. Not knowing their intended victim by sight, they assumed Edwards was the driver who had called in sick.

According to later testimony, the Klansmen "slapped him around a bit," and threatened to castrate Edwards, but he consistently denied having made advances to any white woman. They drove Edwards through the countryside for most of the night, harassing him until he was nearly paralyzed with fear.

Then they took Edwards to the Tyler Goodwyn Bridge in Montgomery County and pulled a gun on him. Edwards cried and begged for his life.

"Jump," they said. Edwards saw his only chance of survival in the dark Alabama River below him, and he jumped.

A fisherman found the decomposed body of Willie Edwards floating in the river three months later.

A CASE TWICE CLOSED

A brief investigation turned up no murder suspects, and the case was closed. Then, 19 years later, Alabama Attorney General William Baxley was investigating several other civil rights cases, and he learned about the murder of Willie Edwards.

After hearing a confession from Raymond Britt, one of the Klansmen at the scene of the crime, Baxley charged Sonny Kyle Livingston, Henry Alexander, and James York with first degree murder.

The case never made it to trial. Alabama Judge Frank Embry twice quashed the indictments, ruling that they did not specify a cause of death. "Merely forcing a per-

1957

Above. Dynamite bombs ripped through four churches one Sunday morning after Montgomery buses were ordered integrated. No one was hurt in the explosions. **Below.** Klansmen tried to intimidate boycotters by walking down Montgomery sidewalks in 1956, but the boycott continued until blacks finally won the right to sit where they chose on the buses.

son to jump from a bridge does not naturally and probably lead to the death of such person," he said.

The prosecutors objected to the judge's ruling, pointing out that the body was too decomposed to determine an official cause of death. But the judge stuck to his decision, and the case was dropped. ■

Mack Charles Parker
1936 -1959

"If we set back and waited for the government to prosecute and punish Mack Parker, it would never happen. So we did it ourselves."

– Mississippi state official

When Mack Parker was arrested for the rape of a white woman in 1959, a Mississippi state trooper offered his pistol to the woman's husband so he could shoot Parker on the spot. Jimmy Walters recoiled at the suggestion. His wife was not even certain that Parker was her attacker, he reminded the officer.

Few white people in Poplarville, Mississippi shared the Walters' sense of justice. So strong was the cry for revenge against Parker that a judge said he couldn't guarantee Parker's safety, and the county jailer started burying the jail keys in his backyard at night. A local newspaper editor wrote, "We have never believed in mob violence, but if M.C. Parker is found guilty of this crime no treatment is too bad for him."

Mack Charles Parker, at 23, had served two years in the Army and was

innocent or guilty of the crime.

PRESUMED GUILTY

Most white people in Poplarville were convinced Parker was the rapist. A former deputy sheriff was among many who believed Parker did not even deserve a jury trial, and he recruited a lynch mob from men attending a prayer meeting.

Three days before Parker was to stand trial, eight masked white men dragged him from his jail cell, beat him, shot him in the heart and threw his body in the Pearl River, where it was found 10 days later. In addition to the former sheriff, the lynch mob included a Baptist preacher and the jailer (who had been persuaded after all to give up his keys).

Within hours, most white people in Poplarville knew Parker had been killed, and they knew who did it. But when FBI agents began investigating the lynching, no

working as a truck driver when he was arrested for the rape of June Walters. He lived with his mother, brother, sister and nephew in a poor black section of Lumberton, Mississippi. He spent most of his wages on the family. On the night of the rape, he had been out with friends. It will never be known whether he was

one in town would tell them anything. Many were afraid of the mob; others simply believed the lynching was justified. The county prosecutor himself praised the lynching and said he would refuse to prosecute anyone arrested for the crime.

Elsewhere, officials were not so ready to set aside the standards of justice. U.S.

Attorney General William Rogers called the lynching a "reprehensible act," and pledged a full investigation. Civil rights leaders said the South's tolerance of vigilante violence proved the need for national legislation against racist killings. Newspaper editorialists throughout the country denounced the lynching.

The negative publicity only enraged whites in Poplarville, and they took their anger out on Mack Parker's family. After receiving a barrage of death threats, Parker's mother Liza fled in fear to California.

the state's action "a travesty of justice," and ordered the Justice Department to build a federal civil rights case. But a federal grand jury also refused to indict. The lynch mob went free.

The verdict was more than a victory for the killers of Mack Parker; it was a victory for the white South over federal interference. Since 1954, Mississippi had led the South in white resistance to integration. The state even had a Sovereignty Commission to combat "encroachment…by the federal government." Soon after Parker's

She was on a bus heading west when her son's body was found. After an American flag was used to drape Mack Parker's coffin, whites raised such an uproar that the Veteran's Administration, which had issued the flag, ordered Parker's sister to return it.

MURDER CONDONED

Finally, persistent FBI agents came up with hard evidence against members of the lynch mob, including several confessions. The evidence was turned over to state prosecutors so they could bring murder charges.

True to his word, the county prosecutor refused to present FBI evidence to the state grand jury, and there were no indictments. U.S. Attorney General Rogers called

death, Governor J.P. Coleman said he hoped Mississippi would not be "punished by civil rights legislation" as a result of the incident.

Some plainly viewed the lynching as an act of heroism against a federal government that was slowly destroying the Southern way of life. As a Mississippi State Sovereignty Commission official put it: "If we set back and waited for the government to prosecute and punish Mack Parker, it would never happen. So we did it ourselves." ■

Opposite Page. Mack Parker's service in the U.S. Army entitled him to be buried in a flag-draped coffin, but whites reacted with such outrage that the Veteran's Administration ordered Parker's sister to return the flag they had given her. **Above.** Liza Parker and her young children mourned the death of her son Mack, shortly before she was forced to leave Mississippi to escape white harassment.

Herbert Lee
1912 -1961

Herbert Lee at age 50 was a small, graying man who had worked hard to build his cotton farm and dairy into a business that would support his wife and their nine children. He had little formal education and could barely read. His wife taught him how to sign his name after they were married.

Lee was a quiet man. Even those who knew him well do not recall hearing him talk about civil rights. But his actions spoke: he attended NAACP meetings at a neighboring farm without fail, even when threats and harassment kept many others away.

Lee's perseverance was one thing that made him valuable to the civil rights movement. Another was his automobile — he was one of the few local blacks with a car of his own. When Bob Moses of the Student Nonviolent Coordinating Committee (SNCC) came to Mississippi in 1961 to register black voters, Herbert Lee was his constant companion. Lee spent hours driving Moses and E.W. Steptoe, the local NAACP president, from farm to farm so they could talk to blacks about voting.

In all of Amite County, there was only one black registered to vote, and that person had never actually voted. Most of the people Moses talked to were not enthusiastic about trying to register, and he quickly learned why. The first time Moses accompanied three blacks to the courthouse to fill out registration forms, he was arrested and spent several days in jail. On his next trip to the courthouse, Moses was beaten by a cousin of the Amite County sheriff. Then another SNCC worker was pistol-whipped and arrested for bringing blacks to a neighboring county courthouse.

After the beatings, no black person was willing to go to the courthouse to register. Most of them also stopped coming to NAACP meetings. Still, Herbert Lee and Bob Moses kept traveling and encouraging blacks to vote. Prince Estella Lee told her husband over and over again to be careful. She recalled later, "he never said anything, he kept on going. A lot dropped out but he kept on going."

Moses sent detailed reports on the attacks to John Doar, an attorney with the U.S. Department of Justice in Washington. Doar was so disturbed by the accounts that he came to Amite County in September 1961 to investigate for himself. Moses took Doar to E.W. Steptoe's farm and Doar asked Steptoe for the names of people whose lives were in danger because of their voting rights activities. Herbert Lee was first on the list Steptoe gave him. Doar looked for Lee, but Lee was away from his farm on business. Doar flew back to Washington.

The next morning, Herbert Lee pulled up to a cotton gin outside Liberty with a truckload of cotton. Several people watched as Mississippi State Representative E.H. Hurst approached Lee and began to shout. Lee got out of the truck and Hurst ran around in front of the vehicle. Hurst then took a gun out of his shirt and shot Lee in the head.

TROUBLED WITNESS

As Lee's body lay on the ground, a white man walked up to Louis Allen, a black farmer and timber worker who had seen the shooting. "They found a tire iron in that nigger's hand," the man said to Allen. Louis Allen knew Lee had no weapon, but he also knew he would be risking his life to say otherwise. So when he was taken to the courthouse to testify before a coroner's jury, Louis Allen lied, and said he saw Lee threaten Hurst with a tire iron.

Those who knew about Lee's voter registration efforts had no doubt that he was murdered. Ten days after his death, 115 black high school students marched through the streets of McComb, Mississippi, to protest the killing.

Louis Allen was tormented by guilt. The 42-year-old father of four told his wife Elizabeth and Bob Moses that he lied about the tire iron to protect himself and his family, but now he wanted to tell the truth. "He didn't want to tell no story about the dead," said Elizabeth Allen, "because he couldn't ask them for forgiveness."

Moses told a Justice Department official that if they could give Allen protection, he would testify to what he saw. The

Louis Allen
1919 -1964

When Bob Moses (left) first came to Mississippi in 1961 to register black voters, he depended on Herbert Lee to be his guide. Moses and Lee spent hours traveling from farm to farm talking to blacks about voting. Although he was anguished by the deaths of Lee and Louis Allen, Moses continued his efforts to register black voters in Mississippi.

government could offer no protection, the official said, and Hurst would probably be acquitted even if Allen did tell the truth.

Allen remained silent to protect his family. And for two years, he lived in constant fear. White customers quit buying logs from him and businessmen cut off his credit. He was beaten in jail after being arrested on false charges. He was told countless times that his children's lives were in danger. He stayed in Amite County only because his mother was ailing and needed him.

Then, only days after his mother died, Allen began making plans to take his family and move to Milwaukee, where his brother lived. The day before he was set to leave — January 31, 1964 — Allen went to a local farmer to obtain a work reference. On his way home he was followed by two cars.

At the bottom of his long gravel driveway, Allen stopped to unlatch the gate. As soon as he got out of his truck, he saw or heard something that frightened him, and he immediately dove under the truck. He was hit with two loads of buckshot in the face. Allen's son Henry discovered the body of his father when he returned home that night from a dance.

No one was ever arrested for the murder of Louis Allen. A reporter later asked a SNCC worker if Allen had been active in the movement. The worker said, "He had tried to register once, and he had seen a white man murder a Negro who tried. In south Mississippi, that made him active." ■

Cpl. Roman Ducksworth Jr.
1934 -1962

pl. Roman Ducksworth was worried and exhausted, but his 950-mile bus ride was almost over. Within hours, he expected to see his wife and their newborn child. The birth had been difficult and his wife and the baby (their sixth) were still in the hospital. Ducksworth, a military policeman, had obtained emergency leave from his post at Fort Ritchie, Maryland. He was sleeping in his seat as the bus finally pulled into his hometown of Taylorsville, Mississippi.

Minutes later, Ducksworth was dead from a gunshot in the heart. Several different accounts of the killing have survived; none of them fully explain what happened or why.

A few facts are clear: Ducksworth was asleep when the bus stopped and a Taylorsville police officer, William Kelly, came aboard. Kelly woke Ducksworth by slapping or hitting him, and ordered Ducksworth off the bus. Then he hit him several more times and shot him.

NO FREEDOM RIDER

Officially, the killing was ruled "justifiable homicide." Officer Kelly claimed Ducksworth attacked him, forcing him to shoot in self-defense, and the grand jury cleared Kelly of any wrong-doing.

However, according to an NAACP investigation, Ducksworth was killed "because he insisted on his rights to sit where he chose on a bus."

In fact, Ducksworth may never have had the chance to argue about his bus seat. He was attacked because "they thought he was a Freedom Rider," speculated Ducksworth's older brother Lee. When he finally tried to defend himself (instead of passively absorbing the blows as the Freedom Riders were taught

to do), he was shot.

During the previous summer, blacks and whites had ridden bravely together on interstate buses and sat side by side in "whites only" waiting rooms and coffee shops. In Alabama, they walked peacefully into the midst of white mobs who brutally attacked them while police stood by. In Jackson, Mississippi, they were taken straight from the bus into police custody.

Roman Ducksworth boarded the bus in Jackson after traveling the same roads the Freedom Riders had taken — through North and South Carolina, Georgia, Alabama and Mississippi — at a time when the Freedom Riders were the most hated of all civil rights activists. But he had little interest in civil rights issues the day he was killed. He was simply a soldier in a hurry to get back home.

THE YOUNGEST SON

Ducksworth was an achiever, but not an activist. He was the youngest of 12 children — nine boys and three girls — whose father was known as a generous friend to both blacks and whites. Roman Ducksworth Sr. farmed 80 acres of land, had served as superintendent of the Cherry

Grove Baptist Sunday School for four decades, and was a reliable source of financial help in bad times.

Eight of the Ducksworth children served in the armed forces. Between

them, Lee Ducksworth recalled, they served all around the globe, but after their tours were over, "we all wanted to come back" to Mississippi. "We loved our home. We farmed and had to work hard, but we enjoyed it."

Roman Ducksworth Jr. had managed to take his wife and children with him during much of his Army career, including three years he spent in Germany. Then, as the family grew, he built a house for them

to Roman Ducksworth Sr., saying, "If I'd known it was your son I wouldn't have shot him."

The elder Ducksworth sent a message back, replying, "I don't care whose son it was, you had no business shooting him."

Ducksworth was buried with full military honors, including a 16-gun salute, at a ceremony attended by an integrated honor guard. ∎

in Taylorsville, and he made plans to move back there after he had completed 10 years of service. He had only a few months of duty to finish when he died.

The killing of Roman Ducksworth shocked both whites and blacks who had known his family for generations. More than 2,000 people attended the funeral. Even William Kelly, the officer who killed him, sent a message by way of his pastor

Opposite page. Freedom Riders traveled the South in the summer of 1961 to test new laws that allowed blacks equal access to bus stations.

Above. Blacks who rode buses were not free of harassment even after the federal government outlawed segregated facilities for interstate passengers. Some Southern cities defiantly ordered facilities for intrastate riders remain segregated.

Paul Guihard
1932 -1962

"It's difficult to believe that you are in the center of the most serious constitutional crisis ever experienced by the United States since the War of Secession."

– Paul Guihard

When James Meredith tried to enroll in the University of Mississippi in the fall of 1962, he was turned away by Governor Ross Barnett, who vowed no black person would attend the state's most prestigious white college.

Barnett did not have the authority to exclude Meredith, a federal court ruled, but the governor would not back down. After negotiations between federal and state officials failed, President Kennedy finally sent in federal troops to ensure the safe enrollment of James Meredith. The stage was set for a battle at Ole Miss, and reporters from all over the world came to cover the story.

One of them was Paul Guihard, a French reporter based in New York City. The day Meredith was to enroll — Sunday, September 30, 1962 — was supposed to be a day off for Guihard, but his editors said the story in Mississippi had to be covered.

CIVIL WAR CONTINUED

Guihard was a tall, husky red-bearded bachelor known for his energy and enthusiasm and nick-named 'Flash' by fellow reporters. When he arrived at the airport in Jackson, Mississippi, a flight attendant who discovered he was French asked, "What are you doing in Jackson?"

"Can't you guess?" replied Guihard.

The woman paused, then said in surprise, "Oh, yes, it's because of that Negro story."

Before Guihard was even out of the airport, he saw the signs of a battle that had become not only a racial crisis but a contest between the highest levels of state and federal government. Several young men were handing out postcards addressed to President Kennedy which urged him to end "the war against nature which he is leading against the sovereign state of Mississippi."

In Jackson, Guihard discovered that a white mob had cordoned off the governor's mansion to protect Gov. Barnett from what they believed was a federal invasion. Guihard described the scene to his French readers as "absolutely unreal,"

in his dispatch that afternoon:

"It is an atmosphere not of crisis but of a carnival…there are thousands of Confederate flags…They are fixed to the radio antennas of automobiles, they are in the buttonholes of men's suits. They are shown by the ladies…and there's a feeling of relaxation in the crowd…People are not at all aware of the enormity of their gesture, of its repercussions and of the interest it is creating all over the world.

"It's difficult to believe that you are in the center of the most serious constitutional crisis ever experienced by the United States since the War of Secession."

Then, as the crowd began to sing "Dixie" and a member of the White Citizens Council bellowed that "A Negroid America will lose her greatness!" Guihard felt the tension rise. He wrote, "It is in these moments you feel there is a distance of a century between Washington and the

segregationists of the South…The Civil War has never ended."

BATTLE OF OLE MISS

Guihard left Jackson for Oxford that day with a sense that he had entered an absurd but slightly terrifying drama.

At the campus of Ole Miss in Oxford, 300 federal marshals were stationed around the main building, where hundreds of angry whites had gathered to await James Meredith's arrival. (Meredith in fact had already been secretly taken to a dorm room, and was under the protection of armed guards throughout the night.)

About 8 p.m., just as President Kennedy announced on national television that the crisis at Ole Miss was resolved, a federal marshal was hit with a lead pipe by someone in the white mob, and a shower of rocks, bricks and bottles came down on the troops. The marshals responded with tear gas. The whites began firing guns.

Less than an hour later, Paul Guihard was found dead in front of a women's dormitory, killed by a bullet in the back.

By morning, the marshals had been

It is not known who shot Guihard, or whether the killer knew he was a reporter. But it was not uncommon for reporters covering civil rights crises to become victims themselves. During the Freedom Rides, white mobs lashed out at reporters and cameramen who were attempting to document the violence. In Birmingham and Selma, reporters were also attacked. But they

continued to bring the news of the civil rights movement to the nation.

Paul Guihard was buried October 5 in Saint Malo, France, following a memorial service in New York attended by U.S. and French officials. President Kennedy expressed his apologies to the French press agency in a telegram, and the University of Mississippi student newspaper set up a scholarship fund in Guihard's name.

Within two weeks after Guihard's death, 20,000 troops were brought into Oxford to maintain calm.

James Meredith's life at Ole Miss was marked by isolation and harassment, but his graduation day came without further violence. Four years later, Meredith was shot and seriously wounded during a one-man march through Mississippi. ■

Opposite page. White men began gathering on the afternoon of September 30, 1962 to try and prevent James Meredith from enrolling in Ole Miss.
Above and left. National Guard troops used tear gas against the violent mob in front of the main building of Ole Miss. By night's end, two people were dead, 200 others had been arrested and dozens of weapons had been confiscated.

reinforced by Army and National Guard troops and nearly 200 people had been arrested. Weapons confiscated from the white mob included more than 40 shotguns as well as rifles, knives, and blackjacks. Of the 300 marshals, 28 had been shot, and 130 others were injured. A white man, Ray Gunter, was found dead from stray gunfire.

William Moore
1927 -1963

A group of black students stood in line at a whites-only movie theater in Baltimore in the winter of 1963, waiting to buy tickets but expecting to go to jail. Sure enough, the police arrived and began arresting the students one by one for trespassing. In the midst of the black students the police were astonished to see a white man, Bill Moore. A puzzled officer asked Moore if he understood that he was in line to be arrested. Moore explained simply that if the others couldn't see the movie because of the color of their skin, then he didn't want to see it either. He spent that night in jail.

No one in Bill Moore's hometown of Binghamton, New York, was surprised at his willingness to go to jail. Moore was known for standing up for his beliefs, even when he stood alone (as he usually did). One time Moore had braved 16-degree weather to walk alone for hours in front of a Binghamton courthouse carrying a sign that read, "Turn Toward Peace."

A RARE IDEALIST

Although he had served with the Marines on Guam in World War II, Moore was a pacifist. He had a degree in social sciences, and had studied in England and France. After his return to the United States, Moore suffered a mental breakdown. He voluntarily entered an institution where he received therapy and worked on a book. The book, called *The Mind in Chains*, was a frank account of his breakdown and recovery. He left the institution after 20 months, healthy but forever aware that he was different from others.

Moore's first mission upon re-entering society in 1954 was to help others like himself. He started one of the first self-help groups for recovering mental patients. Then he took a job as a social worker. Before he left that job, he had given nearly $3,000 of his own money to his clients.

Bill Moore was gifted, some would say cursed, with a reflexive conscience — one that automatically recognized human need and automatically responded to it. Moore

knew that people laughed at his idealism, but he was never ashamed of it. He married a woman who appreciated his uniqueness and gave him confidence to pursue his dreams.

When he left Binghamton for Baltimore, he joked with reporters about his image as a "nut" and said he hoped his protests would have more impact in his new home.

In Baltimore, Moore worked as a substitute mail carrier and devoted his free time to writing and demonstrating. Although he joined a local Congress of Racial Equality (CORE) group, Moore never fit comfortably into the civil rights organizational mold. He cared little about political strategies. He felt individuals could be agents of social change simply by acting on their beliefs.

To make his point, Moore used a tactic that seemed natural for a postman: he walked. He walked alone from Baltimore to the state capitol in Annapolis to protest segregation. Later he walked to Washington, D.C., to deliver a letter to President Kennedy at the White House. (A guard there told him to put the letter in a mailbox.)

Undaunted, Moore made plans for a much longer walk — from Chattanooga, Tennessee, to Jackson, Mississippi — to deliver a letter in which he urged Governor Ross Barnett to accept integration.

THE LAST WALK

Moore had little encouragement for his march to Jackson. CORE, which had sponsored the bloody "Freedom Rides" two years earlier, withheld support from Moore's march because their leaders considered it too dangerous and too limited to be effective. Even Mary, Moore's wife, tried to discourage him.

When Moore wrote to relatives in the South about his plans, they responded with bitter criticism. One aunt wrote back saying, "Our home will be closed to you on a trip of this nature…You'll probably find out when you hit this section of the South what you are doing is not a joke after all." She signed off, "With love, and a prayer to God that he will deliver you from this thing that has taken possession of you."

Moore had been raised by grandparents in Mississippi, and still felt a strong connection to the region. He tried not to take his aunt's criticism personally, and he didn't let it stop him.

Wearing pro-integration signs and wheeling a postal cart full of clothes, he left Chattanooga on April 21, 1963. Shortly after he crossed the Alabama state line on the first day of his journey, he was accosted by motorists screaming "Nigger-lover!" and throwing rocks. He wrote casually about the incident in his journal and he apparently had no fear.

The next day, he befriended a stray dog that followed him. By the end of that day his feet were blistered, and the next day's walk was painful.

Just south of Colbran, Alabama, a white store owner named Floyd Simpson heard about a man who was wheeling a postal cart and wearing signs about integration, and he decided to go find him. Moore was happy to stop for a while and explain his views on racial equality to Simpson.

Later, Moore stopped at a grocery store and gave his tag-along dog to some children there. On his way down U.S. Highway 11 toward Reece City, he stopped on the roadside to rest. He made his last journal entries: "Feet sore all over. Shoes too painful…Kids adopt dog."

As he was resting by the road that evening, Moore was killed by bullets fired at close range from a .22-caliber rifle. Ballistics tests later proved the rifle belonged to Floyd Simpson, but no one was ever indicted for the murder.

In death, Moore earned the public credibility that had never been his in life. Alabama Governor George Wallace and President Kennedy denounced the killing. Civil rights organizations held marches and memorial services. Within a month, 29 young people were arrested in Alabama for trying to finish the walk begun by William Moore. They were carrying signs that read, "Mississippi or Bust." ■

APRIL 23

1963

Opposite page. William Moore relied on the support of his wife Mary during his lonely protests.
Left. Students who never knew William Moore joined to complete the march he began. Many of them were arrested and went to jail.

Medgar Evers
1925 -1963

*In Jackson,
Mississippi, in 1963,
There lived a man
who was brave.
He fought
for freedom
all of his life,
But they laid
Medgar Evers
in his grave.*

—Bob Dylan,
"The Ballad of Medgar Evers"

By the time Medgar Evers was 28, he had lost a family friend to a lynch mob. He had been turned away from a voting place by a gang of armed white men. He had been denied admission to a Mississippi law school because he was black. Nevertheless, Medgar Evers loved Mississippi. He fought in World War II for the United States "including Mississippi," he told people. And he returned from overseas with a commitment to steer his home state toward civilization.

That determination and a great deal of personal courage would carry him through many trials during the next nine years. Evers became the first NAACP Field Secretary for Mississippi, and he spent much of 1955 investigating racial killings. Evers' research on the murders of George Lee, Lamar Smith, Emmett Till and others was compiled in a nationally distributed pamphlet called *M is for Mississippi and for Murder.*

There was immense danger and little glory attached to civil rights work in Mississippi — even for the NAACP's highest state official. Medgar Evers was the one who arranged the safe escape of Mose Wright after the elderly black man risked death to testify against the white killers of Emmett Till. It was Medgar Evers who counseled James Meredith through the gauntlet of white resistance when Meredith became the first black person to enroll at the University of Mississippi. When there were no crises to respond to, there were long hours on the road organizing NAACP chapters.

In the Spring of 1963, Evers was living in Jackson, leading a drive for fair employment and integration against a stubborn city government. When Evers sent a list of black demands to Mayor Allen C. Thompson, the mayor replied in a televised speech to blacks: "You live in a beautiful city," Thompson said, "where you can work, where you can make a comfortable living...do not listen to false rumors which will stir you, worry you and upset you...."

The mayor's speech only angered blacks more. The television station granted Evers equal air time. "History has reached a turning point, here and over the world," Evers said. He compared black life in Jackson to the lives of black Africans. "Tonight, the Negro knows...about the new free nation in Africa and knows that a Congo native can be a locomotive engineer, but in Jackson he cannot even drive a garbage truck...."

The bold speech made Evers the focus of racial tensions in the city. Young blacks became more impatient as city officials stubbornly refused to listen to civil rights demands. On May 28, an integrated group of students sat quietly at a white lunch counter while white thugs sprayed them with paint and poured salt and pepper on their heads. A photo of the incident was published nationwide, and Mayor Thompson was suddenly forced to negotiate with black leaders. During the series of meetings and demonstrations which followed, Medgar Evers became a hero to blacks in Jackson and a mortal enemy to whites.

TENSIONS RISE

As the momentum of the movement increased, so did the threat of violence. A molotov cocktail was thrown at Evers' house. Student demonstrators were beaten by police. So many protesters were arrested that the state fairground had to be turned into a detention camp. Evers spent day and night in negotiations and strategy sessions, seeking desperately to avoid violence.

Then, on the night of June 12, 1963, President Kennedy delivered his strongest message ever on civil rights. "We face…a moral crisis as a country and a people," Kennedy said. "A great change is at hand, and our…obligation is to make that revolution, that change, peaceful and constructive for all."

Evers watched the presidential address with other NAACP officials. Greatly encouraged, they held a strategy session lasting late into the night. When Evers finally arrived home, it was after midnight. He pulled into his driveway, gathered up a pile of NAACP T-shirts reading "Jim Crow Must Go," and got out of his car.

Myrlie Evers had let her children wait up for their father that night. They heard his car door slam. "And in that same instant, we heard the loud gunfire," Mrs. Evers recalled. "The children fell to the floor, as he had taught them to, and I made a run for the front door, turned on the light and there he was. The bullet had pushed him

forward, as I understand, and the strong man that he was, he had his keys in his hand, and had pulled his body around the rest of the way to the door. There he lay."

Neighbors lifted Evers onto a mattress and drove him to the hospital, but he was dead within an hour after the shot.

The next morning, police discovered a small clearing in a patch of honeysuckle near the house. On the ground nearby lay a high-powered rifle with a telescopic sight. An FBI investigation later showed the fingerprints on the rifle belonged to Byron De La Beckwith, a charter member of the White Citizens Council. Beckwith was tried twice for murder — both trials ended in

hung juries and he was never convicted.

RAGE CONTAINED

Myrlie Evers had often heard her husband counsel forgiveness in the face of violence. But the night he was killed, there was only room for grief and rage in her heart. "I can't explain the depth of my hatred at that point," she said later. The next night, with newfound strength, she spoke before 500 people at a rally. She urged them to remain calm and to continue the struggle her husband died for.

Others were unable to contain their anger. On June 15, after more than 5,000 people had gathered in silent tribute to Evers, a group of black youths began singing and marching in defiance of a court order. Police and fire engines confronted them on a downtown street, and the youths began throwing rocks. Several police officers drew their pistols. John Doar, a Justice Department lawyer who had come to attend Evers' funeral, knew there was going to be a riot unless someone acted quickly. Doar walked in between the police and demonstrators and urged the youths to turn back. They obeyed, and there was no violence.

Four days later, Evers was buried in Arlington National Cemetery. A military bugler played "Taps" and the crowd of 2,000 sang "We Shall Overcome."

The day after Evers' funeral, Mayor Thompson appointed the city's first black police officer, as part of an agreement reached with black leaders in the aftermath of Evers' murder. Although the settlement was not a complete victory for Jackson's black citizens, it was a major step toward the goals for which Medgar Evers had fought.

A year before his death, Evers told an interviewer why he devoted his life to the struggle for civil rights: "I am a victim of segregation and discrimination and I've been exposed to bitter experiences. These things have remained with me. But I think my children will be different. I think we're going to win." ■

Opposite page. Black youths angered over the assassination of Medgar Evers confronted police in a tense moment after Evers' funeral. Violence was avoided only after John Doar, a U.S. Justice Department lawyer, stepped in.

Left. The body of Medgar Evers was laid to rest in Arlington National Cemetery on June 19, 1963. Myrlie Evers and two of her three children, Darrell Kenyatta, 9, and Reena Denise, 7, are seated at right.

Addie Mae Collins
1949 -1963

Denise McNair
1951 -1963

It was Youth Sunday at Sixteenth Street Baptist Church in Birmingham, Alabama. The preacher had prepared a sermon especially for the children. The youth choir would lead the congregation in music, and children would serve as ushers.

For the youngsters, many of whom had marched proudly with Dr. Martin Luther King Jr., it was another in a series of momentous events that year. That spring, their own church had been the center of a campaign against segregation. The long struggle was won mainly because children were brave enough to march into the overpowering water hoses and vicious dogs of Police Commissioner Bull Connor. After television news cameras revealed the brutal force unleashed on the children, city officials were forced to reform their harsh segregation laws.

Now lunch counters were no longer closed to blacks, and a federal court had just ordered white schools in the city to admit black children. The whole world had watched in awe as the children in Birmingham made history. Before this day was over, the whole world would mourn.

THE SACRIFICE OF CHILDREN

In the basement ladies' lounge of Sixteenth Street Baptist Church, four girls were chatting nervously and straightening their fancy white dresses. In a few minutes, the worship service would begin. Addie Mae Collins, 14, and Denise McNair, 11, were in the choir. Carole Robertson and Cynthia Wesley, both 14, had been chosen to serve as ushers.

Only a few feet away, beneath a stone staircase along the outside wall of the church, a dynamite bomb had been planted eight hours earlier. At 10:22, it exploded. The whole church shook. Plaster and debris fell around the people in Sunday School upstairs. The four girls in the ladies' lounge were killed instantly.

For a few minutes, there was only screaming and chaos. Then people began to search through the rubble for victims. In the end, more than 20 people were hospitalized with injuries. One of them was Addie Mae Collins' sister Sarah, who was blinded in one eye.

There had been many bombings in Birmingham designed to stop the black struggle for equality. Ministers' homes, a black-owned hotel, and other churches had been wrecked. But there had been nothing so evil as the dynamiting of children during Sunday School. The news spread quickly, and it sickened people of all races and all political allegiances throughout the world.

Civil rights leaders tried to channel the grief and rage that spread through the black community, but there was little comfort in their efforts. Gangs of black and white youths battled in the street, and businesses went up in flames.

Martin Luther King Jr. had delivered his "I Have a Dream" speech to the largest civil rights march in history only 18 days earlier. Now he spoke quietly to a crowd of 8,000 at a joint funeral for three of the bomb victims.

"God still has a way of wringing good out of evil," he told the mourners. "The innocent blood of these little girls may well serve as the redemptive force that will bring new light to this dark city...Indeed,

this tragic event may cause the white South to come to terms with its conscience."

'WE ALL DID IT'

The FBI immediately investigated the bombing, and discovered it was planned by Klansmen in response to the new school desegregation order. An eyewitness saw four white men plant the bomb. Unexplainably, no one was charged with the crime.

Then, 14 years later, Alabama Attorney General William Baxley reopened the case.

Opposite page. While police and firemen began investigating the bombing of 16th Street Baptist Church, an empty stretcher awaits one of the victims.
Left. The explosion ripped through the church and damaged nearby automobiles.

Cynthia Wesley
1949 - 1963

Carole Robertson
1949 - 1963

A 73-year-old Klansman named Robert Chambliss was charged with first-degree murder, and the jury found him guilty. Chambliss was sent to prison, where he died. No one else has ever been tried for the Sixteenth Street bombing.

September 15, 1963 was remembered as a day of victory for the Klan. Shortly after the church bombing, white supremacist leader Connie Lynch told a group of Klansmen that those responsible for the bombing deserved "medals." Lynch said the four young girls who died there "weren't children. Children are little people, little human beings, and that means white people … They're just little niggers…and if there's four less niggers tonight, then I say, 'Good for whoever planted the bomb!' "

The Sixteenth Street bombing, perhaps more than any other event of the period, brought national attention to the evil of racism. The tragedy sparked a surge of support for federal civil rights legislation, and it led to an intensive voting rights campaign in Selma, Alabama.

But more importantly, it made the pain of racism felt among whites who would never experience it themselves. The day after the bombing, a white lawyer named Charles Morgan gave a speech in Birmingham. He asked his audience: "Who did it?" and gave his own anguished answer: "We all did it…every person in this community who has in any way contributed…to the popularity of hatred is at least as guilty…as the demented fool who threw that bomb." ■

Virgil Lamar Ware
1949 -1963

When violence erupted in the aftermath of the Sixteenth Street church bombing, Chris McNair, father of the youngest victim, pleaded for calm:"We must not let this change us into something different than who we are. We must be human."

A s members of the bombed Six-teenth Street Baptist Church waited with the wounded and grieving at the hospital on September 15, 1963, the streets of Birmingham erupted. Some blacks, who had struggled through months of threats and violence during the campaign for civil rights, could no longer contain their rage. They threw rocks at police and gangs of white boys, and set fire to several white businesses.

The families of the four dead girls tried to stop the violence. Chris McNair, the father of the youngest victim, said, "We must not let this change us into something different than who we are. We must be human."

Yet, even as black leaders pleaded with their followers not to meet violence with violence, two other black youths were killed that day.

A 16-year-old boy, Johnny Robinson, was among a crowd of black youths who were throwing rocks. When the police arrived, the youths turned to run. The police fired shotguns at them. Robinson was killed by a load of buckshot in the back.

In a suburb of Birmingham, 13-year-old Virgil Ware was riding on the handle-bars of a bicycle while his older brother James pedaled. It was Sunday afternoon; neither of them had heard about the bombing yet. As James brought the bike down Docena Road, they were approached by two white boys riding a red motorscooter decorated with Confederate stickers. The boy riding on the back of the motorscooter pulled out a .22-caliber pistol and fired twice without saying a word.

Virgil was hit in the chest and the face. He fell from the handlebars to the ground and died.

The killers of Virgil Ware were quickly identified. They were Michael Lee Farley and Larry Joe Sims, both 16, Eagle Scouts, and regular churchgoers. They confessed to the killing but told the police they didn't know why they shot Virgil Ware.

An investigation showed that Farley and Sims had attended a segregationist rally before the shooting. They had also visited the headquarters of the National States Rights Party (NSRP), a white supremacist group whose members had been involved in bombings and other racial violence. The NSRP taught that black people were less than human, and they didn't deserve to live in America. Farley and Sims, indoctrinated in such fanatical racism, killed Virgil Ware casually, as if they were shooting at an animal.

The white youths went to trial — not for murder, but for the lesser charge of manslaughter. They were convicted and sentenced to seven months in prison. But Joe Sims, the boy who pulled the trigger, was released after only a few days in custody. The trial judge set him free and warned him not to have another "lapse." ∎

1963

"The innocent blood of these little girls may well serve as the redemptive force that will bring new light to this dark city…Indeed, this tragic event may cause the white South to come to terms with its conscience."

– Dr. Martin Luther King Jr.

"They're just little niggers…and if there's four less niggers tonight, then I say, 'Good for whoever planted the bomb!'"

– White Supremacist Leader Connie Lynch

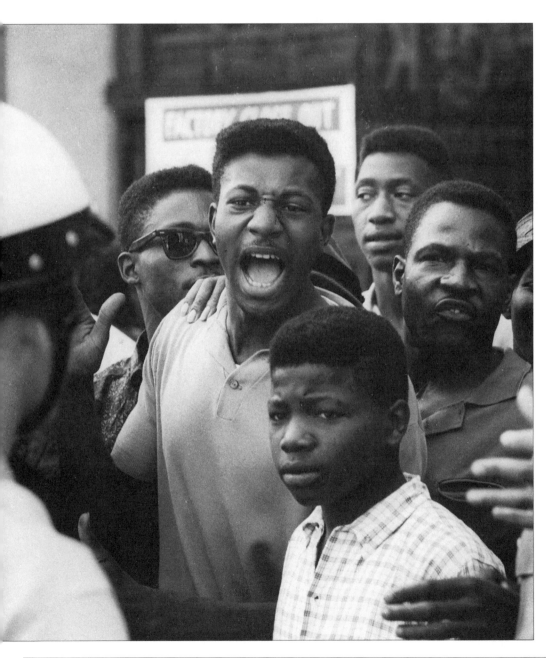

Angered by the murder of four schoolgirls in the 16th Street Church bombing, black youths took their rage to the streets. Although the outburst was short-lived, two more young people were killed before the day was over.

Rev. Bruce Klunder
1937 -1964

"I pray that by the time the children grow up, their father's death will have been redeemed, and they will be able to see the effect of what his dying did for the consciences of at least a few people — at least a few."

–Joanne Klunder

Bruce Klunder was a minister who believed his life must be his sermon. He was living out his faith when he laid his body down in the mud behind a bulldozer that was breaking ground for a segregated school. Klunder's intention was not simply to protest segregation, but to prevent it. Instead, he was crushed to death. And although his death was in one sense an accident, it was also an expression of the purpose to which he had committed his life.

In 1955, when blacks in Montgomery stopped riding buses to protest segregation laws, Klunder was an 18-year-old college student in Oregon, far removed from the realities of racism. The bus boycott awakened him to the inequities between blacks and whites in America. Klunder raised money to help support the Montgomery boycotters and he began discussing civil rights issues with his fellow YMCA Student Council officers. His mission had begun.

After completing Divinity School at Yale, Bruce and his wife Joanne moved to Cleveland where he took a job with the Student Christian Union and immediately immersed himself in civil rights issues. He and Joanne took a group of students on a field trip through the South to expose them to the effects of segregation, and they became founding members of the Cleveland chapter of the Congress of Racial Equality (CORE). Klunder was among the CORE members who demonstrated at the state legislature for a fair housing bill. Whenever there was a protest against injustices in housing and education, Klunder was there.

For Bruce Klunder, this work was not just a matter of conscience. His hope was not simply to improve black lives, but to make his own life an expression of God's love. Before he was killed, Joanne remembered, they talked about moving their family into the heart of the ghetto "so that our children could grow up knowing the meaning of caring for others."

WE ALL ARE ONE

Bruce Klunder articulated his beliefs in a 1963 sermon in which he told the white congregation that it was not enough for Christians to bring fairness and equality into their personal relationships: they must also work to reform the institutions of society — even if it meant taking personal risk.

"Our central affirmation is that, through Jesus Christ, we all are one — one with God and one with each other…We must — each in his own way — suffer with and for those who are oppressed by those structures of injustice…We must learn to feel their pain as our own and…be willing to bear personally some of the cost of that pain's removal."

One of the institutional injustices that blacks suffered all over the country was inadequate education. In Cleveland, black schools were so old and overcrowded that students had to attend classes in shifts. White schools were lavish in comparison, with an abundance of teachers and books.

When civil rights leaders in Cleveland protested the overcrowded conditions in black schools, the school board agreed to send a number of black students to white schools. But white parents objected that they didn't want their children going to integrated schools. Bowing to white pressure, the school board agreed to build more schools for black children, so white schools would not have to be integrated. Local ministers and civil rights leaders were outraged that school officials would go to such lengths to preserve segregation.

LIVES ON THE LINE

Bruce Klunder and others were determined to stop the construction of the black schools. When legal roadblocks failed, they staged picket lines at the site of the first school. When police began arresting demonstrators, some of the protesters decided to place their own bodies in the way of construction equipment. "We will not stop short of having the school board revise its plans," said Klunder.

On April 7, Klunder and several others went to the construction site where a bulldozer was preparing ground for the black school. Three protesters threw themselves to the ground in front of the bulldozer. Bruce Klunder went to the back of the vehicle and laid down on the muddy ground. When the bulldozer operator reversed directions to move away from the protesters in front, the huge machine ran over Klunder, crushing him to death.

Police ruled the death an accident. Some blacks in the community reacted with rage and were on the brink of rioting when Joanne Klunder made a plea for calm. The violence was sporadic and

Even after the Supreme Court outlawed segregated schools, cities all over the country sought ways to preserve Jim Crow facilities. In most cases, school integration came only after civil rights activists insisted on equal rights for black children.

short-lived.

In the aftermath of Klunder's death, school officials halted construction on the segregated school. Once tensions eased, however, the work was resumed and the school was completed.

Joanne Klunder wrote later that her husband's death shook whites and blacks out of a sense of complacency about racial injustice. "There now is a feeling of 'Yes, we can do something about it — and we must.' "

She continued, "I pray that by the time the children grow up, their father's death will have been redeemed, and they will be able to see the effect of what his dying did for the consciences of at least a few people — at least a few." ◼

Charles Eddie Moore
1944 -1964

Henry Hezekiah Dee (photo unavailable)
1945 -1964

The South's most dangerous Klan organization, the Mississippi White Knights, planned a violent response for Freedom Summer. Charles Moore and Henry Dee were their first victims.

They called it Freedom Summer. For many, however, the summer of 1964 would be remembered as a season of terror.

It was the year that hundreds of college students, recruited from Northern campuses in a highly publicized campaign, came to work in rural Mississippi. They started Freedom Schools to teach black children about their rights and their heritage. They coached adults through the hurdles of voter registration procedures. And they brought national attention to the repression and poverty that enslaved black people in Mississippi.

They also confronted a force of white resistance more brutal than any of them had imagined — the kind of terrorism that had haunted blacks in the South for generations.

COUNTERATTACK ON CIVIL RIGHTS

Even before Freedom Summer began, members of the South's most violent Klan organization, the Mississippi White Knights, were planning their response. They began by burning 64 crosses on a single April evening throughout Mississippi. By June, the White Knights had established 29 chapters with an estimated 10,000 members.

On May 3, White Knights Imperial Wizard Sam Bowers issued what amounted to a declaration of war against the Freedom Summer workers: "The events which will occur in Mississippi this summer may well determine the fate of Christian civilization for centuries to come," Bowers wrote in his Imperial Executive Order to all White Knights members. Bowers urged his members to conduct "counterattacks" against "selected individual targets."

A month and a half later, White Knights murdered James Chaney, Andrew Goodman, and Michael Schwerner in one of the most widely publicized atrocities of

the entire civil rights movement.

By the end of the summer, 80 people had been beaten, 35 shot at, 5 murdered, and more than 20 black churches had been burned to the ground in Mississippi alone. Much of the violence could be traced to members of the White Knights.

Although the murders of Chaney, Goodman, and Schwerner received worldwide attention, two other White Knights victims went practically unnoticed. They were Charles Moore and Henry Dee, young black Mississippians who had disappeared in early May. Their mutilated bodies were discovered in the Mississippi River during the massive search for the three civil rights workers.

FORGOTTEN VICTIMS

Maisey Moore last saw her son Charles talking to Henry Dee on May 2. Moore, 20, had just been expelled from college for taking part in a student demonstration. He had gone into Meadville to look for work. Dee, 19, worked at a local lumber company and lived with his grandmother in a shanty near the Homochitto National Forest.

When Moore did not come home that night, his mother assumed he had gone to Louisiana to look for a job. When he still had not returned in two days, Mrs. Moore notified the sheriff. A few days later, the sheriff told Mrs. Moore that the two were staying with one of Dee's relatives in Louisiana. Unconvinced, Mrs. Moore and the sister of Henry Dee drove to see the relative. Charles Moore and Henry Dee were not there and never had been.

More than two months later, on July 12, 1964, a man fishing in the Mississippi River near Tallulah, Louisiana, found the lower half of a badly decomposed body. The body was dressed in jeans and the ankles were tied with rope. FBI agents rushed to the scene, suspecting the body might be one of the missing civil rights workers. The search continued, and the

truck driver, was the son of a White Knights chapter leader. Edwards worked at the International Paper Company in Natchez, a center of White Knights activity.

Edwards gave the FBI a signed confession. Moore and Dee had been murdered, he explained, because the White Knights believed they were Black Muslims plotting an armed uprising of local blacks. Dee was suspected because he had once lived in Chicago; Moore because he had participated in a student demonstration. (In fact, the Black Muslim plot was a wild, unfounded rumor.)

In his confession, Edwards described the killing. The White Knights abducted Moore and Dee from a roadside and took them deep into the Homochitto National Forest, where they tied them to trees and beat them unconscious. Then the Klansmen loaded their victims into a car and drove to the Louisiana side of the Mississippi River. After tying heavy weights (including a Jeep motor block) to their bodies, they threw them in.

The FBI gave Edwards' confession along

Opposite page. Rescuers dragged Mississippi rivers in a massive search for three civil rights workers who disappeared in June 1964. The bodies of Charles Moore and Henry Dee were discovered during the search.
Left. Klansmen thought they would be able to stop the civil rights movement by intimidating blacks. When masked confrontations did not work, they resorted to violence.

next day a second body was discovered. This one was decapitated and a piece of wire was wrapped around the torso.

A school key was found in the jeans on the first body, identifying it as Charles Moore. The second body was identified as Henry Dee.

Two White Knights members — James Ford Seale, 29, and Charles Marcus Edwards, 31 — were arrested for the murders. Seale, a

with other evidence to state prosecutors, who were responsible for bringing murder charges. But a Justice of the Peace promptly dismissed all charges against the White Knights, without explanation and without presenting the evidence to a grand jury. ■

James Chaney
1943 - 1964

Andrew Goodman
1943 - 1964

Michael Schwerner
1939 - 1964

Mount Zion Methodist Church had stood solid since the turn of the century, but by Sunday, June 21, 1964, nothing was left except a pile of bricks and ashes, a few charred hymnals, and the church bell.

Three young civil rights workers — Michael Schwerner, James Chaney and Andrew Goodman — stood amid the rubble, staring dismally at what would have been their first Freedom School. Church members had only reluctantly agreed to make their building available for civil rights activities for fear that something like this would happen.

Now their church was in ruins; several of their members had been beaten by Klansmen; and the three civil rights workers were in danger. The Klansmen who burned the church had been looking for Mickey Schwerner.

TARGETED

Schwerner, a 24-year-old social worker from New York City, had worked in Meridian for the Congress of Racial Equality (CORE) since January and had become accustomed to threats. For the Klan and its sympathizers (including many local law enforcement officials), Schwerner was despised as a symbol of the civil rights invasion that was threatening their way of life. They hated him for his friendships with local blacks, for his attempts to challenge segregation, and not least, for his open disregard for Southern standards of appearance: he wore a short beard at a time when no respectable Southern man wore facial hair.

The White Knights of the Ku Klux Klan, who nicknamed Schwerner "Goatee," had plotted to kill him as early as March, but their attempts so far had failed.

Schwerner's closest associate, James Earl Chaney, had helped convince Mount Zion members to host the Freedom School. Chaney, 21, had grown up in Meridian as the oldest son of a domestic servant and a traveling plasterer. "J.E." as his family called him, had once been suspended from school at age 16 for wearing an NAACP button. By the time he went to work with CORE he knew better than to broadcast his civil rights views. He rarely discussed his activities, even with his closest friends. It was a reckless line of work for a black Southerner, and Fannie Lee

Chaney was worried for her son.

But Chaney was invaluable to CORE. He knew every back road, every farmhouse in the county, and he was behind the wheel when he and Schwerner left the church ruins that Sunday.

The third person in the car with them was Andrew Goodman, an anthropology major from New York who was spending his first day in Mississippi as a volunteer for the Mississippi Summer Project. Goodman had participated in one of the earliest civil rights marches in Washington when he was only 14. At age 16, he had picketed a Woolworth's store in New York City in support of the Southern sit-ins.

TRAPPED

When Chaney, Goodman, and Schwerner left the church that afternoon, they headed toward Philadelphia, Mississippi. At the town limits, they were stopped by Neshoba County Deputy Sheriff Cecil Price. Price arrested Chaney for speeding and Goodman and Schwerner for the arson of Mount Zion church. (The ludicrous charge was a familiar ploy of whites who claimed civil rights workers staged their own violence to create sympathy for their cause.)

The arrests of Chaney, Goodman, and Schwerner set a long-awaited plan into motion. Klansmen immediately began gathering at the home of a member in Meridian. Job assignments were handed out, directions given, meeting times coordinated. Three Klansmen were sent out to buy rubber gloves. Another was assigned to contact a local bulldozer operator.

Deputy Price jailed the civil rights workers without letting them use the telephone. Then, about 10 o'clock that night, he suddenly released them and ordered them to return to Meridian. Chaney, Goodman, and Schwerner had not gone far before Price pulled them over again. This time, he was accompanied by two carloads of Klansmen.

Chaney was struck with a blackjack as soon as he stepped out of the car. All three were ordered into the back seat of Price's patrol car, then driven to an isolated spot off Highway 19. One by one, the three young men were taken out of the car and shot at point-blank range. Their bodies were deposited at a nearby farm where an earthen dam was under construction. The

1964

Top. The burned car of the missing civil rights workers was found in the Bogue Chitto swamp, where Klansmen had hidden it.
Bottom. Deputy Sheriff Cecil Price (left) and Sheriff Lawrence Rainey (right) at their trial. Price was found guilty of federal civil rights violations in the murder of the three civil rights workers and Rainey was acquitted.

bulldozer operator who had been hired by the Klan scooped out a hole for the bodies, and built the dam above them.

The disappearance of the three civil rights workers sent shock waves throughout the world. Within hours after their disappearance, top officials at the U.S. Justice Department were notified. Within days, President Johnson met with the parents of Goodman and Schwerner. By the end of the week, 100 FBI agents were assigned to search for the missing men.

Despite widespread talk about the abduction and killings, no one in Neshoba County would tell the FBI what they knew. Some suggested the murders were a CORE publicity stunt. Others said the three men were troublemakers who got what they deserved. One local white woman spoke out against the murders and lost her Sunday School teaching job as a result. "It has made me understand how Nazi Germany was possible," said Florence Mars.

The search for the three civil rights workers quickly became the biggest federal investigation ever conducted in Mississippi. The FBI dragged 50 miles of the Pearl River and marched in columns through the

This page. Ben Chaney stands with his mother and father at a memorial service for his older brother James.

Opposite page. Mothers of the slain civil rights workers — Mrs. Chaney, Mrs. Goodman and Mrs. Schwerner (left to right) — link arms after the funeral service for Andrew Goodman in New York City.

swamps looking for the bodies. Agents interviewed 1,000 people and built up a 150,000-page case file.

Finally an anonymous informer revealed the location of the bodies in exchange for $30,000 in federal reward money. The next day, a team of FBI agents and a hired bulldozer dug up 10 tons of soil to uncover the decomposed bodies of Chaney, Goodman and Schwerner. They discovered Chaney had been shot three times. In the tightly clenched fist of Andy Goodman they found a handful of soil from the dam.

Thousands of mourners and civil rights leaders attended services for Mickey Schwerner and Andrew Goodman in New York City.

At a Baptist church in Meridian on August 7, veteran CORE worker Dave Dennis rose to speak at James Chaney's funeral. The typically quiet man, known as an intellectual, looked down to see James' younger brother Ben crying in the front row, and he was filled with rage. Countless black people, like James Chaney, had given their lives during the struggle for equality. Now, because two whites were among the victims, the world paid attention.

Dennis reminded the crowd of the martyrs who had gone before: Emmett Till, Mack Parker, Herbert Lee, Medgar Evers. And he said, "I'm not going to stand here and ask anyone not to be angry, not to be bitter tonight!" Dennis struggled to control his voice. "I'm sick and tired, and I ask you to be sick and tired with me. The best way we can remember James Chaney is to demand our rights...If you go back home and sit down and take what these white men in Mississippi are doing to us...if you take it and don't do something about it...then God damn your souls!"

In the months that followed, several Klansmen gave information to the FBI, but no charges were brought until civil rights activists sued for the legal right to prosecute the suspects. Finally, the U.S. Justice Department called a federal grand jury and won indictments against 19 men, including police officials and Klansmen, for the murders.

On October 20, 1967, seven Klansmen, including Samuel Bowers and Deputy Price, were found guilty of federal civil rights violations in the deaths of the three men. They were sentenced to prison terms ranging from three to 10 years. Three other defendants were freed by a hung jury, and three were acquitted.

It was the first time a jury in Mississippi had ever convicted Klansmen in connection with the death of a black person or civil rights workers. ◼

Lt. Col. Lemuel Penn
1915 -1964

One week after Chaney, Goodman, and Schwerner were murdered in Mississippi, Lemuel Penn left his home in Washington D.C., for two weeks of Army Reserve training in Georgia. Penn was familiar with Southern segregation after years of summer training at Fort Benning. He was also a cautious man. In the violent summer of 1964, he spent the entire two weeks of Reserves training on base just to avoid any possible racial confrontations.

When it came time to return North, Penn timed his trip so that he and two fellow black officers could drive through the night without having to stop. Their tour of duty was up at midnight on Friday July 10. Fifteen minutes later Penn left, accompanied by Maj. Charles E. Brown and Lt. Col. John D. Howard. They brought sandwiches and soft drinks with them and carried no weapons.

A LIFE OF CHALLENGES

Penn, 48, was known as a brilliant educator and a dignified man — a "magnificent gentleman," as his fellow officers described him. He served in the South Pacific during World War II, and by 1964 was a lieutenant colonel in the Reserves.

Although he was not involved in the civil rights movement, Penn had filled his life with challenges. He started out teaching math and science in an all-black school, and now was head of vocational education for the integrated Washington D.C., school system. He had received the Boy Scouts' highest leadership award for establishing a camp for black children. His wife Georgia was also a teacher, and they

lived with their three children in a quiet integrated neighborhood.

The night before he left Fort Benning, Penn telephoned his wife to let her know when to expect him home. There had been daily reports of racial violence in the South that summer, but Penn assured his worried wife that he was in no danger.

Four hours into their trip home, the officers stopped to change drivers. Penn took the wheel. A few minutes later, about 22 miles from Athens, Georgia, he saw he was being followed by a speeding station wagon. At about 4:45 a.m. the station wagon, with three white men in it, overtook Penn. As it passed, two loads of buckshot blasted through the side windows of the officers' car. One entire load hit Penn in the neck, killing him instantly.

The other two officers struggled to move Penn's body aside and regain

control of the car. The pursuing car forced them into a ditch, then sped off.

Both the Army and the FBI began investigating the Penn murder immediately. The more questions they asked, the more it seemed that the crime was the work of Klansmen.

KLAN TERROR

The Athens chapter of the Klan had a "security force" called the Black Shirts, that combatted civil rights efforts by terrorizing blacks. In March of 1964, they beat up a 50-year-old black mechanic. In June they fired shots into a black housing project, blinding a 19-year-old in one eye.

The Klansmens' obsession with vio-

lence was only strengthened in early July when President Lyndon Johnson signed a law providing broad civil rights protection to blacks. Only nine days later, Lemuel Penn was dead.

An Athens Klansmen named James S. Lackey confessed to the killing. He said he drove the car carrying two fellow Klansmen, Cecil William Myers and Joseph Howard Sims. "The original reason for our following the colored men," Lackey said, "was because we heard Martin Luther King might make Georgia a testing ground for the civil rights bill. We thought some out-of-town niggers might stir up some trouble in Athens."

When they spotted the black officers, Lackey recalled, Sims said: "That must be some of President Johnson's boys." As the chase began, Sims told Lackey, "I'm going to kill me a nigger." When Lackey pulled alongside the other car, Sims and Myers fired simultaneously.

Lemuel Penn was buried with full military honors at Arlington National Cemetery. His body was borne to its grave on the same horse-drawn caisson that carried the body of President John F. Kennedy only eight months earlier. Shortly before the funeral, Georgia Penn had said she hoped her husband's death would lead to more concern about racial violence.

Sims and Myers were first tried for murder and acquitted by an all-white jury. In the months following their acquittal, they were arrested for attacking a black photographer during a civil rights demonstration and for beating a one-legged black farmer they had run off the road.

U.S. Justice Department officials were alarmed by the actions of Southern courts in cases of racial violence, and they looked for other ways to prosecute Penn's killers. Finally, they charged Sims and Myers and four other Klansmen with conspiring to violate the civil rights of blacks by intimidation and harassment. A district judge promptly threw out the federal indictment. Determined federal prosecutors appealed the decision to the U.S. Supreme Court. The Court reinstated the indictment in an important ruling that allowed broader federal enforcement of such conspiracies.

When the federal case against Sims and Myers went to court in June of 1966, prosecutors brought in three cartons of weapons confiscated from the Klansmen. There were sawed-off shotguns, pistols, clubs with swastikas carved in them, and a heavy chain welded to a swivel handle. Prosecutors detailed a two-year pattern of violence by the Klan "security force" which climaxed in the slaying of Lemuel Penn.

In response, the attorney defending the Klansmen argued that his clients "may be guilty of a little violence, even a little bad violence," but they were only trying to "help out" by "letting the colored people of Athens know that somebody else other than the police was watching them."

In the end, Myers and Sims were convicted of the civil rights violations and given the maximum 10 prison sentences. The four other Klansmen were acquitted. It marked only the second time that the federal government had successfully prosecuted a case of civil rights conspiracy. ■

Opposite page. Two loads of buckshot crashed through the car carrying three Army Reserve officers. Lemuel Penn, who was driving, was killed instantly.

Left. Klansman Joseph Howard Sims (in handcuffs) was sentenced to 10 years in prison for civil rights conspiracy in the killing of Lemuel Penn.

Jimmie Lee Jackson
1938 -1965

"Jimmie Lee Jackson's death says to us that we must work passionately and unrelentingly to make the American dream a reality. His death must prove that unmerited suffering does not go unredeemed."

– Dr. Martin Luther King Jr.

In 1962, when civil rights organizer Albert Turner persuaded some black residents of Marion to try and register to vote, an elderly farmer named Cager Lee was one of the first in line at the courthouse.

Standing with Lee was his daughter, Viola Lee Jackson, and her son Jimmie Lee Jackson. They were not permitted to register. When Jimmie Lee Jackson saw his frail 80-year-old grandfather rudely turned away from the registrar's office, he became angry. He knew that he must be a part of the movement for civil rights.

Years earlier, when he was a proud high school graduate of 18, Jimmie Lee Jackson had made plans to leave rural Alabama for a better life in the North. He abandoned those dreams when his father died, leaving him to run the family farm. Determined to make the most of his life, Jackson took logging work in addition to farming, and he became active in a local fraternal lodge. At age 25, he was the youngest deacon ever elected at his church.

After the incident at the courthouse, Jackson saw the chance for real change in his hometown of Marion. He wrote a letter to a federal judge protesting the treatment of black voter applicants. He attended civil rights meetings, participated in boycotts of white businesses, and joined others in marching for the right to vote.

In nearby Selma, activists had been marching for voting rights since early 1963. In January of 1965, they were joined by Martin Luther King Jr., who brought national attention to the voting rights campaign. King led nightly mass meetings and frequent marches to the courthouse, where demonstrators were turned away by a stubborn Sheriff Jim Clark.

During one week in February, more than 3,000 marchers were arrested in Selma. On February 10, the sheriff's posse used cattle prods to drive the marchers all the way out of town, leaving them stranded and injured about a mile from the city limits. And on February 16, Sheriff Clark clubbed civil rights leader C.T. Vivian and

then arrested him after Vivian continued to argue for the right to vote.

As the Selma campaign heated up, so did activity in Marion. On February 3, Marion police arrested 700 black children for marching around the courthouse and jailed a civil rights leader for contributing to the delinquency of minors.

ATTACK AT NIGHT

The combined resistance of Alabama officials angered the Marion demonstrators, and they decided to step up their campaign with a tactic they knew would be dangerous: night marches.

The day after he was released from jail in Selma, C.T. Vivian went to Marion to lead a mass meeting and night march. About 9:30 the night of February 18, more than 200 marchers began walking in pairs out the front door of Mount Zion church. Before they had even walked a block, they were confronted by a line of state troopers and the police chief, who ordered them to disperse.

The marchers halted at the chief's order, and suddenly all the street lights on the square went out. A black minister at the head of the march knelt to pray, and was struck on the head by a trooper. Other troopers began swinging their clubs and the marchers panicked, running for cover wherever they could find it.

Viola and Jimmie Lee Jackson hurried into Mack's Cafe and were huddled for safety when they saw Cager Lee come in, beaten and bleeding. Shocked at the sight of his grandfather wounded, Jimmie Lee tried to lead him out the door to take him to a hospital. But they were quickly shoved back into the room by a crowd of club-swinging troopers and terrified marchers.

The troopers began knocking out the cafe lights with their clubs and beating people at random. Jimmie Lee saw a trooper strike his mother, and he lunged for the man without thinking. A trooper clubbed him across the face and slammed him into a cigarette machine. As Jimmie Lee was forced against the machine, another trooper pulled his pistol and shot him in the stomach.

Wounded, Jimmie Lee managed to escape the cafe, but the troopers continued

to beat him as he ran up the street. Eventually he collapsed. It was two hours before Jimmie Lee arrived at Good Samaritan Hospital in Selma. He died eight days later.

Jackson's killer was never publicly identified and no charges were ever brought. Three days before Jackson died, the Alabama state legislature passed a resolution supporting the state troopers' actions in Marion.

TEST OF NONVIOLENCE

The death of Jimmie Lee Jackson, at the hands of a man sworn to uphold the law, put the followers of nonviolence to a tremendous test. In the past 18 months, they had seen five murders in Alabama and six in Mississippi. Just five days before Jackson died, black leader Malcolm X had been assassinated.

There was no disguising the bitterness civil rights activists felt at the death of Jimmie Lee Jackson. Albert Turner, who had started the voting rights drive in Marion,

said, "We were infuriated to the point where we wanted to carry Jimmie's body to (Alabama Governor) George Wallace and dump it on the steps of the Capitol."

It was a testament to the genius of the nonviolent gospel and its ministers that such bitterness did not explode in a rage of violence. At one of two services for Jackson, Martin Luther King told a crowd of 2,000:

"Jimmie Lee Jackson's death says to us that we must work passionately and unrelentingly to make the American dream a reality. His death must prove that unmerited suffering does not go unredeemed. We must not be bitter and we must not harbor ideas of retaliating with violence. We must not lose faith in our white brothers."

Yet more than encouraging words would be needed to calm the surge of grief and rage. James Bevel, an associate of King's, thought a long march from Selma to Montgomery would help absorb the tension in the movement and bring national publicity to the problem of voting rights.

Thousands of blacks and whites from all over the country gathered in Selma on March 21, 1965 to march behind Dr. Martin Luther King Jr. to the state Capitol in Montgomery. Jimmie Lee Jackson's grandfather, Cager Lee, was one of the first in line.

By the time the Selma to Montgomery march was completed, two other civil rights workers were dead. The murders of James Reeb, Viola Liuzzo and Jimmie Lee Jackson made voting rights a matter of national urgency. Three months after the Selma march, Congress passed a broad voting rights bill and federal officials began the massive job of registering blacks throughout the South. ∎

Left. The hearse carrying the body of Jimmie Lee Jackson drove slowly through the rain as an estimated 700 people followed.

Opposite page. Hundreds of voting rights activists were arrested in Marion during February 1965.

Rev. James Reeb
1927 -1965

The gathering in Selma of white people from all over the country was a sensational boost for local blacks who had been marching steadily for two years. It proved to the sheriff who hated them, the troopers who beat them, and the governor who denounced them that people everywhere shared their cause.

From the time he was a boy, James Reeb followed his conscience. He spent his teen-age years working with disadvantaged youth. He felt called to the ministry even before he graduated from high school. As a Unitarian minister in Washington D.C., Reeb spent more time helping the poor people who lived near the church than he spent in church. By 1965, Reeb was living with his wife and three children at the edge of a Boston ghetto and devoting his life to improving slum conditions.

On March 7, 1965, Reeb watched in horror as television news showed the attack by Alabama state troopers on civil rights marchers in Selma. The next day, when Martin Luther King Jr. sent out a nationwide plea for ministers of all races and religions to come to Selma, James Reeb knew he had to go.

Reeb's wife Marie, who was accustomed to her husband's unconventional choices, told him this time that she wished he wouldn't go to Selma. A fellow minister warned him, "you could get hurt." But Reeb saw the decision as one of conscience, and felt he had no choice.

That night, James Reeb was among hundreds who flew into Montgomery, Alabama. From there it was a short drive to Selma and by 9:00 a.m. on March 9, Reeb and ministers from all over the nation were in Selma, ready to march. They expected this to be a brief, jubilant demonstration of unity, and most of them planned to fly home the next day.

The gathering in Selma of white people from all over the country was a sensational boost for local blacks who had been marching steadily for two years. It proved to the sheriff who hated them, the troopers who beat them, and the governor who denounced them that people everywhere shared their cause.

MARCH HALTED

Then a federal judge ordered the march postponed. With 2,000 people waiting to march, King could not tell them all to go back home. They started out from Brown Chapel on the morning of March 9. James Reeb walked near the back, his arms linked with another clergyman and a black man from Selma. When the front ranks reached the line of troopers waiting for them, King gave the signal to retreat. He had never defied a federal court order, and could not bring himself to put the marchers in any more danger.

At Brown Chapel that night, King explained to the marchers why they had retreated. But he asked the people from out of town to stay awhile if they could, and promised there would be a march to Montgomery.

James Reeb was among those who decided to stay. That night, after eating at a local black cafe, Reeb and two other ministers made a wrong turn as they were walking down the street. Strangers to Selma, they began heading toward the Silver Moon Cafe, a notoriously rough all-white club. They heard shouts: "Hey, you niggers!" and saw four white men approaching. One of the men swung a heavy club into the side of Reeb's head, sending him crashing to the ground. Then the gang knocked the other two down and kicked them. "That's how it feels to be a nigger down here," the attackers said before they left.

Reeb managed to get up from the blow, but he had an agonizing headache. The next few hours were a nightmare of mishaps as his condition worsened. Doctors at the local infirmary told Reeb to see a neurosurgeon in Birmingham, but the hospital there required an entrance fee, so the ministers had to wait until the $150 fee could be collected. On the way to Birmingham, their ambulance had a flat tire and they had to wait for another one — and this one's siren was broken. It was 11 p.m. before Reeb finally arrived at the hospital. He had a massive skull fracture and a large blood clot. He died two days later.

There was a surge of national outrage at Reeb's death, in sharp contrast to the official silence that accompanied the death of Jimmie Lee Jackson. Memorial marches were held all over the country. The President phoned Marie Reeb, and the Vice President attended Reeb's funeral.

Jimmie Lee Jackson's mother had received no such attention when she lost her son, and the reason, most believed, was race. Reeb was white; Jackson was black. No one in the movement questioned the value of Reeb's sacrifice; they only wished Jimmie Lee Jackson's had been similarly recognized.

Nevertheless, it was Reeb's death more than anything else that focused the national spotlight on Selma.

"It's a terrible thing to say, but it took the death of a white clergyman to turn things around," remembered Orloff Miller, one of the ministers who was attacked with Reeb. "When James Reeb, a white clergyman from the North, was killed in Selma,

people suddenly sat up and took notice and from then on things changed in the movement. People came from all over the country to Selma."

Four days after Reeb died, President Johnson delivered a voting rights bill to Congress. In a nationally televised speech Johnson said the struggle in Selma "is part of a larger movement...Their cause must be our cause, too. Because it's not just Negroes but really it's all of us who must overcome the crippling legacy of bigotry and injustice. And we shall overcome."

Those last three words, spoken by the President, sent shock waves throughout the white resistance and brought tears to the eyes of civil rights activists. It was a sign that even white leaders, far removed from the battlefronts, were learning the lesson James Reeb had understood from the beginning: this was a struggle that demanded a commitment from all who loved justice, regardless of their color.

Reeb's death, like Jackson's and so many others, went unpunished. Although four white men were arrested and indicted, it took a jury only 90 minutes to decide they were not guilty. ▪

Clergy people of all faiths came to Selma to join the voting rights demonstrators after they were attacked by state troopers at the Edmund Pettus Bridge. Finally, protected by federal troops, thousands completed the march to the Alabama state Capitol on March 25.

Viola Gregg Liuzzo
1925 -1965

"We (pray) for rest, peace and light to Mrs. Liuzzo. Maybe she has finally found a life free of prejudice and hate."

On the evening of March 25, 1965, while civil rights marchers were making their way back to Selma after the climax of their three-day march, a white man who had participated in the beating of James Reeb sat in the Silver Moon Cafe talking to a group of Klansmen. "You boys do your job," the man said. "I already did mine."

The Klansmen, a select group from a klavern near Birmingham, had been sent to Selma with orders to keep the marchers "under surveillance." After leaving the cafe, they headed out of town toward Montgomery. At a stoplight, they noticed a green Oldsmobile with Michigan license plates driven by a white woman with a young black male passenger. That car symbolized for them the two most despised aspects of the civil rights movement: outsiders and race-mixing. The Klansmen had found their target.

Viola Liuzzo, a 39-year-old white mother from Michigan, was still full of energy after three long days of shuttling marchers between Montgomery and Selma. A stranger when she arrived in Selma six days earlier, she had become known as a tireless and cheerful worker. A priest from Chicago who had been on the march said, "Her energy, enthusiasm and compassion were contagious and put many of us to shame."

Mrs. Liuzzo sang strains of the civil rights anthem, "We Shall Overcome," as she turned her Oldsmobile back toward Montgomery for another carload of marchers. LeRoy Moton, a young black man, was riding with her to help drive. Moton was surprised at her nonchalance when they discovered they were being followed by a carload of white men. "These white people are crazy," Mrs. Liuzzo said, and pressed the accelerator.

Soon both cars were racing down the highway at 100 miles per hour. About 20 miles outside Selma, on a lonely stretch of road in Lowndes County, the carload of

Klansmen pulled up alongside Liuzzo's Oldsmobile. Viola Liuzzo turned and looked straight at one of the Klansmen, who sat in the back seat with his arm out the window and a pistol in his hand. He fired twice, sending two .38-caliber bullets crashing through the Oldsmobile window and shattering Viola Liuzzo's skull.

LeRoy Moton grabbed the steering wheel and hit the brakes, and the Oldsmobile crashed into an embankment. The Klansmen came back to inspect their

work, and Moton feigned death while they shone a light in the car. As soon as they left, Moton flagged down a truck carrying more civil rights workers. Moton was terrified but uninjured. Viola Liuzzo was dead.

AN EXTRAORDINARY WOMAN

Viola Liuzzo, by all descriptions, was an extraordinary woman. At age 36, with five children at home, she went back to school to become a medical lab technician. She graduated with top honors, but worked for only a few months before she quit her job in protest over the way female secretaries were treated. With the encouragement of her friend and housekeeper Sarah Evans she became one of the few white members of the National Association for the Advancement of Colored People.

On March 7, 1965, Viola and Jim Liuzzo were watching the 11 o'clock news when they saw the first film clips of state troopers attacking Selma marchers at the Edmund Pettus Bridge. Tears rolled down Mrs. Liuzzo's face as she watched the brutal attack on television. She brooded over the scene for days. Then came the news reports of the death of James Reeb. She got in her car and left for Selma alone, despite her husband's concerns.

After Viola Liuzzo was killed, Jim and

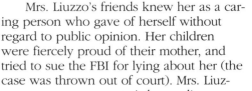

Mrs. Liuzzo's friends knew her as a caring person who gave of herself without regard to public opinion. Her children were fiercely proud of their mother, and tried to sue the FBI for lying about her (the case was thrown out of court). Mrs. Liuzzo's home diocesan newspaper chastised those who criticized her character: "We cannot wish mercy to those who have passed a judgement of hate upon her. They have found the only possible way to alienate a forgiving God…We (pray) for rest, peace and light to Mrs. Liuzzo. Maybe she has finally found a life free of prejudice and hate."

President Johnson was enraged at Mrs. Liuzzo's murder, and he ordered Congress to start a complete investigation of the Ku Klux Klan. That investigation uncovered a series of Klan crimes and led to a curtailment of Klan violence.

Three Klansmen — Eugene Thomas, William Orville Eaton, and Collie LeRoy Wilkins Jr. — were indicted for the murder of Viola Liuzzo. The state had a strong case: the fourth Klansmen in the car, Gary Thomas Rowe Jr., was an FBI informant and he had seen everything. The Klan's attorney defended his clients by delivering a violent harangue against the murder victim herself. The case ended in a hung jury. During the retrial, a second all-white jury deliberated less than two hours before finding the Klansmen not guilty.

Many people, including some federal officials, were becoming frustrated at the consistent failure of Southern juries to convict civil rights opponents. In an unusual move, the U.S. Justice Department decided to bring federal charges against Thomas, Eaton, and Wilkins for conspiring to violate the civil rights of Mrs. Liuzzo. A federal jury found the Klansmen guilty, and Alabama federal district Judge Frank M. Johnson Jr. handed down the maximum prison sentence of 10 years for each defendant. The Liuzzo case became known as a milestone in the history of Southern justice. ■

the children also became victims. They were besieged with hate mail and phone threats. The Klan circulated ugly lies about Mrs. Liuzzo's character, and these were repeated in FBI reports. Though they were proven false, the rumors fueled sentiment among some that Mrs. Liuzzo was out of "her place" in Selma, that she should have stayed home with her children. A *Ladies Home Journal* survey showed that only 26 percent of readers approved of Mrs. Liuzzo's mission in Selma.

Opposite page. Viola Liuzzo tried to outrun the Klansmen who were following her car. When they caught up with her, they fired a .38-caliber pistol through the window, killing her instantly.
Left above. Four of Viola Liuzzo's five children grieve after hearing of the death of their mother. They are (left to right) Anthony, 10, Sally, 6, Penny, 18. and Tommy, 13.
Left below. Selma marchers on their way to Montgomery.

Oneal Moore
1931 -1965

His older brother teased him and his mother worried endlessly, but Oneal Moore could not have been prouder when he was chosen to be one of the first black deputies in Washington Parish, Louisiana. His selection was no surprise to those who knew him. Moore was a 34-year-old Army veteran who had distinguished himself as a leader in his church, his local fraternal lodge and the P.T.A. He had four daughters who idolized him and a wife who had great ambitions for him and their children. Oneal's eight brothers and sisters remembered him as a confident, hard-working youth who treated all people with respect but who would not let anyone take advantage of him.

Moore became deputy in Washington Parish at a dangerous time. The parish was known to have the largest Klan membership per capita of any place in the country, and it was not unusual for carloads of white thugs to ride through black areas shooting at homes and cars. Sheriff Dorman A. Crowe named Moore and another man, Creed Rogers, deputies in response to black demands for more police protec-

tion. The appointments enraged some whites, particularly members of the Ku Klux Klan.

Despite the white animosity, Moore was proud of his appointment. He let his daughters listen to the police radio in his patrol car. When his brother Ameal teased him about being a deputy, Oneal put on his uniform and bashfully told his brother "this ain't no tin badge." Oneal's younger sisters, who had always looked up to him, nearly burst with pride. Only his mother was frightened.

Oneal knew he had put himself and his family at risk by accepting the job, and he tried to be cautious. While other blacks in the area marched and picketed, and some even armed themselves as defense against the Klan, Moore avoided civil rights activities. He wanted only to be able to perform his duty — to protect law-abiding citizens from violence and crime.

AMBUSHED

Exactly a year after they were appointed, Rogers and Moore had finished their nightly patrol and were heading home

1965

Opposite page. Marvella Moore sits between her daughters Tressler (left) and Regenia (right) at the burial of her husband. Oneal Moore's mother and father are seated at left.
Above. A Klansman passes out calling cards in Bogalusa. Washington Parish was known as a center of Klan activity in the mid-1960s.

toward Varnado when their car was hit by a volley of gunfire. Moore was hit in the head and instantly killed. Rogers was wounded in the shoulder and blinded in one eye. As their attackers sped away, Rogers managed to broadcast a description of their car on the police radio.

News of the killing spread quickly, and officials feared there would be more violence. They were right: three days after Moore's death, bullets were fired into the home of a white deputy who was heading the murder investigation. Sheriff Crowe said the shooting was probably the work of white extremists, and he pledged all resources to solve the murder and the shooting. Louisiana Governor John McKeithen offered a $25,000 reward for information leading to the killers of Oneal Moore.

In response to the killing, civil rights activists in Washington Parish stepped up their marches and demonstrations. A black self-defense group called the Deacons for Defense placed armed guards in black neighborhoods. Hundreds of state police were brought in to help prevent violence. Louisiana Governor John McKeithen came to Bogalusa to meet with black activists and white segregationists, urging both sides

to remain calm.

Despite the rage that many blacks felt at the murder of Oneal Moore, Marvella Moore would allow no signs of anger at her husband's funeral. She asked national civil rights leaders attending the funeral to make no public statements. A *New York Times* reporter described the eulogy as "remarkably free of bitterness."

Following the tragedy of Moore's death, civil rights activities increased in Washington Parish. Black boycotts finally succeeded in forcing the integration of restaurants and theaters in Bogalusa. Rural black youth began learning about their rights at Freedom Schools run by the Congress of Racial Equality. And a massive voter registration drive added hundreds of blacks to the voting rolls.

The murder case was never solved. Police arrested a suspect — a man named Ernest Ray McElveen who belonged to several white supremacist groups, including the National States Rights Party, the United Conservatives and the White Citizens Council. However, the charges against him were unexplainably dismissed, and neither McElveen nor anyone else was ever prosecuted for the murder of Oneal Moore. ■

Willie Brewster
1926 -1965

It was the first time during the civil rights era that a white person was convicted of killing a black person in Alabama. The guilty verdict astonished everyone, including civil rights leaders who had already made plans to protest an acquittal.

The National States Rights Party had more in common with the Ku Klux Klan than with a political party. Its claim to fame during the 1960s was a "riot squad" of two men — Connie Lynch and J. B. Stoner — who hated blacks and Jews so much that they became evangelists of violence, traveling the South delivering fanatical racist speeches to whoever would listen.

Although the term "lynch mob" was coined long before Connie Lynch began his escapades, the irony is appropriate. Lynch, who called himself a minister, frankly urged his listeners to "kill the niggers," and sometimes named specific targets in the towns he visited. After Klansmen in Birmingham bombed a church, killing four schoolgirls, Lynch told a white crowd: "If there's four less niggers tonight, then I say good for whoever planted the bomb."

On the night of July 15, 1965, about 100 white people gathered at the courthouse in Anniston, Alabama, to hear Connie Lynch speak. He told the audience there should be a special medal for whoever killed Viola Liuzzo. He promised that all politicians who supported civil rights efforts would be hanged when the National States Rights Party took over the country. He went on to say, "If it takes killing to get the Negroes out of the white man's streets and to protect our constitutional rights, then I say, yes, kill them!"

Sitting at the podium while Lynch spoke was J.B. Stoner, the NSRP lawyer who made a business of defending Klansmen and others charged with racist crimes. Next to Stoner was Kenneth Adams, another NSRP official who owned part of a local oil distribution business, and who once assaulted the famous black singer Nat King Cole at a concert in Birmingham. In the audience was one of Adams' employees, 23-year-old Hubert Damon Strange, and his friend Jimmy Knight.

About the time Lynch's tirade reached its peak, three black men were getting off work from a local pipe foundry. One of them was Willie Brewster, a hard-working 38-year-old who raised his own vegetable garden in addition to working at the factory. When the shift ended on the night of July 15, Brewster got in a co-worker's car for the ride home to Munford, a small town 20 miles from Anniston, where Brewster's pregnant wife Lestine was waiting with their two small children.

Willie Brewster was described by his boss as someone who "went beyond his duties to help." When his friend complained of aching feet during the drive home, Brewster took over the wheel. He was driving down Highway 202 when three gunshot blasts tore through the back window. A bullet slammed into Brewster's spine and he slumped over the wheel. The uninjured riders caught a glimpse of several white men in a passing car as they tried to regain control of their own vehicle.

ENEMIES OF US ALL

For the next several days, Lestine Brewster sat with her husband at the hospital while a local newspaper raised reward money for information leading to his assailants. The reward offer, wrote an

Anniston Star editor, "says to Willie Brewster and to the world that he is not alone at this moment, that the persons who brought him to the point of death…are not just his enemies. They are enemies of us all, and we stand together in opposition to them." Civic leaders raised $20,000 within

1965

12 hours and Alabama Governor George Wallace added another $1,000 to the reward fund.

The doctors told Lestine that if her husband lived, he would be paralyzed from the waist down. Willie tried to reassure his wife, saying, "I'm going to get well." But three days after the shooting, he died. Lestine had to be hospitalized immediately, and a month later she lost her baby through miscarriage.

Three white men — Hubert Damon Strange, Johnny Ira Defries and Lewis Blevins — were indicted for the murder of Willie Brewster on August 27, 1965. Strange, the first to be tried, was represented by NSRP lawyer J.B. Stoner. Jimmy Knight, who had attended the NSRP meeting with Strange, was the star prosecution witness. He testified that he heard Strange boast, "we got us a nigger" after the shooting.

After 13 hours of deliberation and 20 ballots, the all-white jury returned a second-degree murder conviction against Strange and sentenced him to 10 years in prison. It was the first time during the civil rights era that a white person was convicted of killing a black person in Alabama. The guilty verdict astonished everyone, including civil rights leaders who had already made plans to protest an acquittal.

Hubert Strange never served his prison term. While he was free on bond waiting appeal, he got into a barroom brawl with another man and was killed. Johnny Ira Defries was acquitted of murder in a second trial. In 1980 Stoner himself was convicted for the racial bombing of a church in Birmingham. He was released from prison in 1986 after serving several years, and returned to his white supremacist activities. ■

Opposite page. Mourners file past the casket of Willie Brewster.
Left. National States Rights Party leader J.B. Stoner (with microphone) traveled the South encouraging violence against blacks.

Jonathan Daniels
1939 -1965

It was not an easy road that led Jonathan Daniels to the ministry. The son of a doctor and a school teacher in Keene, New Hampshire, Jon had always been active in his church. But his teen-age years were a long storm of rebellion, during which his grades dropped and his parents despaired. Sensing his own need for discipline, Jon attended Virginia Military Institute for his college studies and he graduated with top honors.

Despite his success, something inside him was unfulfilled. During his first year in graduate school at Harvard, Jon was overcome by doubt and depression. Then on Easter Sunday in 1962 he had a religious awakening that changed the rest of his life. He left Harvard and decided to become a minister.

Jonathan Daniels was a 26-year-old student at an Episcopal seminary in Cambridge, Massachusetts, when Dr. Martin Luther King Jr. issued his nationwide call in 1965 for clergy of all faiths to come to Selma to support the voting rights marchers. Daniels knew that he was meant to go to Selma, and he went eagerly.

During the long hours of waiting, meeting, and marching in Selma, Daniels was buoyant in the knowledge that he was living his faith. He made fast friends with a black family who opened their home to him, and he quickly saw the urgent need for economic and political reform in the region. When the thrilling pageant of the Selma-Montgomery march was over, Daniels decided to stay and work in Alabama.

AN ABUNDANCE OF STRENGTH

One of his first goals was to integrate a local Episcopal church. Despite their common creeds, Southern churches were (and most still remain) racially separate. Daniels believed churches should be the first to reach out to people of all races, but his efforts met with stubborn resistance from white churchgoers and ministers.

Daniels soon turned his attention away from reforming white consciences to helping poor blacks exercise their rights. He helped them obtain welfare and farm assistance, encouraged them to register to vote, and tutored many of their children who had inadquate educational opportunities because they were black.

Jonathan Daniels, said a fellow civil rights worker, helped give people the courage they needed to exercise their rights. "He had an abundance of strength that came from the inside that he could give to people," said Stokely Carmichael. "The people in Lowndes County realized that with the strength they got from Jon Daniels they had to carry on, they had to carry on!"

On Saturday, August 14, black teen-agers in Fort Deposit, Alabama, gathered to picket white stores that discriminated. Daniels and two fellow ministers joined in the protest. There were threats of white mob violence, and police had already informed the marchers they would be arrested for their own protection. As the group approached downtown, the police kept their word, and Jon Daniels and Father Richard Morrisroe were among the 30 marchers taken to the jail in Hayneville.

A LICENSE TO KILL

The marchers spent nearly a week in jail, and then suddenly on August 20 they were released without explanation and with no transportation back to Fort Deposit. While one of them went to telephone for a ride, two teen-agers walked with Daniels and Morrisroe toward a nearby grocery store to buy a soda. When they got to the door, they were met by a man with a shotgun who told them to leave "or I'll blow your damned brains out!" In a split second, Daniels pushed one of the teenagers out of the way and the gun went off.

The shot hit Daniels in the stomach, killing him instantly. Morrisroe was hit in the back, critically injured. (Morrisroe eventually recovered after months of hospitalization and physical therapy.)

Tom Coleman, 55, a part-time deputy sheriff of Lowndes County, put down his shotgun, walked over to the courthouse and called Colonel Al Lingo in Montgomery. "I just shot two preachers," he told the state trooper commander. "You better get on down here."

A grand jury indicted Coleman for manslaughter instead of murder, after hearing Coleman testify Daniels had pulled a knife on him. The members of the all-white jury took less than two hours to find Cole-

man not guilty and shook his hand as they filed out of the courtroom.

It was an old and bitter story of Southern justice, but this time even the attorney general of Alabama could not contain his outrage. The acquittal, Richmond Flowers said, represented the "democratic process going down the drain of irrationality, bigotry and improper law enforcement...now those who feel they have a license to kill, destroy and cripple have been issued that license."

Jon Daniels had died without fear, for he knew the dangers of doing civil rights work in the South. He wrote after arriving in Alabama, "I lost fear in the black belt when I began to know in my bones and sinews that...in the only sense that really matters I am already dead and my life is hid with Christ in God." ∎

Opposite page. A Boston seminary student, Jonathan Daniels made himself at home with the children of Lowndes County, Alabama. **Left.** Members of the all-white jury who tried the accused killer of Jonathan Daniels take a break beside a Confederate statue. They took less than two hours to find the accused not guilty.

Samuel Younge Jr.
1944-1966

"This is an era of social revolution. In such revolutions, individuals sacrifice their lives."

— **Samuel Younge Sr.**

Sammy Younge could have had an easy life. He grew up in a prominent middle-class family in Tuskegee, Alabama — a town dominated by a famous black university and noted for its progressive race relations. Younge attended a New England boarding school for a while, and served two years in the Navy. He was a bright, exuberant youth, brought up to have pride in his race and confidence in himself.

Although prosperity and prestige were his, they were not what interested Sammy Younge. He required adventure; and the biggest adventure going on in Alabama in the late 1950s was the civil rights movement. Even as a child, Younge saw the struggle for equal rights as a personal challenge. He was light-skinned enough to pass for white, and he would sometimes fool store clerks or train porters to gain entrance to white facilities, as a way of mocking segregation laws.

REJECTING HYPOCRISY

Sammy Younge entered the prestigious Tuskegee Institute in the fall of 1964 with the intention of getting a degree in political science. But he quickly became dissatisfied with the hypocrisy he saw among black leaders in Tuskegee. While blacks in Birmingham and Montgomery had succeeded in integrating their cities, it seemed the well-to-do blacks in Tuskegee were content to live with segregation and voting abuses as long as their own prosperity was not threatened.

Other students at the Insitute, who had long heard the praises of Tuskegee's racial progress, looked around them and saw blacks being shut out of jobs and turned away from the voter registration office, and black children denied the chance to swim at a public pool in the summertime. They formed the Tuskegee Institute Advancement League (TIAL) to push for stronger reforms. Sammy Younge became one of TIAL's most active members. He participated in boycotts which forced businesses to hire blacks, and worked in successful campaigns to integrate local restaurants and the public pool.

Yet it was the plight of poor rural blacks that most concerned Younge. He had been isolated most of his life from the black farmers outside Tuskegee, but now he felt he had more in common with them

than with his middle-class peers. Soon he was spending more time in the countryside recruiting voters than he was spending in class.

Then Younge began to feel the full impact of white resistance. In the summer of 1965, he was among TIAL students who were beaten while trying to attend a white church in town. Weeks later, someone threatened to blow up the home where Younge's mother lived. Then someone fired shots at a truck he was riding in. Finally, on the first day of September, Sammy Younge was arrested along with about 60 others who were trying to register to vote in Opelika.

CONFRONTATION

The violence and arrests frightened Younge, and when the new school term started he tried to concentrate on his studies. But he could not get the movement out of his blood. When the accused killer of civil rights worker Jonathan Daniels was acquitted in Lowndes County, Alabama, Younge organized a protest march. He even traveled to Lowndes County to help black tenant farmers who had been evicted because they tried to vote.

On January 3, 1966, Younge was back in Tuskegee, organizing blacks to go to the Macon County courthouse to register to vote. (It was one of the two days a month the registrar's office was open.) A man at the courthouse tried to scare him with a knife, but Younge waited until the last voter was registered. By the end of the day, about 100 black voters had been added to the rolls.

That night, there was a party. Younge danced and drank for a while, then went out to buy some cigarettes. At the local service station, he asked to use the restroom and was directed to the back of the station. Convinced he was being sent to a "colored" bathroom, he argued for a moment with the 67-year-old attendant, Marvin Segrest, then left. As Younge walked away from the service station, a shot was fired. He tried to run for cover, but the second shot struck him in the head and killed him.

The murder touched off immediate demonstrations. About 2,000 Tuskegee students and faculty marched through downtown in a steady rain the next day to protest the killing. They were openly

Above. Students carried a mock casket to the White House to protest the killing of Sammy Younge.
Below. Younge was shot to death between this bus station and the Standard Oil station at left.

angry, and they continued to express their rage in demonstrations the following week. The City Council urged students to restore calm, but racial tensions mounted.

Then the man who shot Sammy Younge was found innocent of murder. Marvin Segrest admitted to an all-white jury that he killed Younge, but claimed he shot in self-defense after an argument over the restroom. (In fact the service station did not have segregated restrooms, Segrest said.)

When they heard about the verdict, the students could no longer contain their rage. They set fires on the town square and threw rocks and bottles into store windows.

The threat of further violence finally forced Tuskegee's black leaders to act.

They pushed for, and won, a city ordinance banning discrimination in hotels and restaurants.

But it was the impoverished rural blacks — many of whom registered to vote because of Sammy Younge — who won the biggest victory. In the fall of 1966, they elected Lucius Amerson the first black sheriff in the South since Reconstruction, despite the lack of support from Tuskegee black leaders who felt a black sheriff could not be elected.

Tuskegee was transformed, and Sammy Younge's father was satisfied that his son had not died in vain. "This is an era of social revolution," said Samuel Younge Sr. "In such revolutions, individuals sacrifice their lives." ■

Vernon Dahmer
1908-1966

Ellie and Vernon Dahmer woke to the sound of gunshots and exploding firebombs. Dahmer grabbed a gun and went to his front door. While the fire raged, he stood in his doorway, inhaling the burning fumes and returning gunfire while his family escaped.

By the time he was middle-aged, Vernon Dahmer had overcome the handicaps of racial discrimination and a tenth-grade education to become a wealthy businessman. He owned a 200-acre commercial farm just north of Hattiesburg, as well as a sawmill and a grocery store. Blacks and whites alike had tremendous respect for Dahmer. His businesses provided much-needed jobs for the rural community, and farmers could always count on Dahmer to lend a hand at harvest time.

As Dahmer built his businesses and raised a family of eight children, he never lost sight of the struggle most black Americans faced. He was elected president of the local NAACP and became notorious for urging his friends and neighbors to vote. "If you don't vote, you don't count," many people heard him say. During the violent months of 1964, when Klansmen fired into black homes and burned dozens of churches, Dahmer sat up at night with a shotgun to protect his family. But he did not stop talking about voting.

Members of the White Knights of Mississippi, the state's most violent Klan group, kept a close eye on Dahmer. When Imperial Wizard Sam Bowers spoke to the local klavern about putting a stop to civil rights activity, Vernon Dahmer's name was always mentioned. At one such meeting, according to Klansmen who were there, Bowers said Dahmer was a 'Project 3' or a 'Project 4' if possible. In Klan code language, Project 3 meant arson; Project 4 meant murder.

After the 1965 Voting Rights Act was passed, a new sense of hope led more and more blacks to the polls. On January 9, 1966, Dahmer made a public offer to collect poll taxes for his neighbors so they wouldn't have to go to the courthouse in town. He said on a radio broadcast that he would even pay the taxes for those who couldn't afford it.

That night, Ellie and Vernon Dahmer woke to the sound of gunshots and exploding firebombs. Dahmer grabbed a gun and went to his front door. While the fire raged, he stood in his doorway, inhaling the burning fumes and returning gunfire while his family escaped. When it was over, Dahmer's home and the nearby store were destroyed. Betty, his 10-year-old daughter, was hospitalized with severe burns. Dahmer's lungs were irreparably scorched.

From his hospital bed, Vernon Dahmer said, "I've been active in trying to get people to register to vote; people who don't vote are deadbeats on the state. I figure a man needs to do his own thinking. What happened to us last night can happen to anybody, white or black. At one time I didn't think so, but I have changed my mind." He died shortly afterward.

THE COMMUNITY RESPONDS

The death of Vernon Dahmer and the destruction of his home and store sparked a reaction that must have surprised the Klansmen — for this time white officials and community leaders were genuinely outraged. The Hattiesburg city council set up a relief fund for the Dahmer family, and a white-owned bank made the first donation. Whites and blacks donated furniture, clothes, and materials to rebuild the Dahmer home. Local officials pledged their full resources to solve the crime.

White sympathy did not erase the anger that blacks felt after the murder and arson. A memorial march for Dahmer nearly exploded when demonstrators and police officers got into a pushing match. Young activists began calling for boycotts and pickets, raising the possibility of further violence. However, tensions soon eased when older black leaders presented a list of grievances to city and county officials, demanding equal hiring in public jobs and desegregation in public facilities. Wanting to maintain peace in the aftermath of tragedy, the officials began to make reforms based on the list of grievances.

Dahmer's murder triggered another unexpected response. The federal government, which had shown reluctance in earlier civil rights cases, reacted this time with speed and determination. President Lyndon Johnson sent a telegram to Dahmer's widow Ellie, praising her husband's civil rights activities: "His work was in the best tradition of a democracy — helping his fellow citizens register and vote. His family can be justly proud as his work was a fine example of good citizenship." Johnson ordered an immediate FBI investigation which was to last more than two months. Fourteen Klansmen were eventually charged with arson and murder.

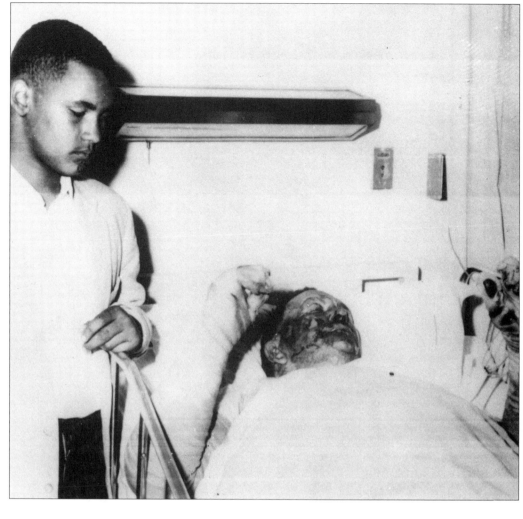

Hospitalized with severe burns, Vernon Dahmer repeated his support for black voting rights shortly before he died. Dahmer's 12-year-old son Dennis is shown here by his father's bedside.

WHITE KNIGHTS ACCUSED

Billy Roy Pitts, a member of the White Knights in Jones County, pleaded guilty to the arson and agreed to testify at the trials of the other accused Klansmen. Over and over, Pitts described how the Klansmen met with Bowers, scouted out the Dahmer residence, filled plastic jugs with gasoline, and then fired shots into the buildings and threw the homemade bombs inside. Pitts lost his pistol at one point during the attack, but Bowers reassured him there would be no problem. "He told me a jury would never convict a white man for killing a nigger in Mississippi."

At one time Bowers would have been right. But times were changing. Three white men — Cecil Victor Sessum, Charles Clifford Wilson and William I. Smith — were convicted of murder and sentenced to life in prison. Bowers and another Klansmen, Henry DeBoxtel, were freed by hung juries. (Bowers was not yet out of trouble — he was convicted of federal civil rights violations in the murders of Chaney, Goodman and Schwerner and was only awaiting the outcome of his appeal before he would be sent to prison.)

Lawyers for the U.S. Justice Department, dissatisfied with the mixed verdicts in the Dahmer case, filed new charges against 11 of the defendants for violating the 1965 Voting Rights Act. A federal jury acquitted three of the defendants and could reach no verdict for the remaining seven.

The trials in the Dahmer case took place over several years. Although they did not result in jail terms for every accused Klansman, they exposed the brutality of the White Knights in Mississippi. Finally, crippled by congressional inquiries, lengthy FBI probes, and the conviction of Bowers, the most violent Klan group in the South fell into disarray. ■

Ben Chester White
1899-1966

Right. Hatred for blacks permeated Mississippi society at all levels. It found expression in atrocities such as the murder of Ben Chester White, and in the sentiment that allowed murderers of blacks to go unpunished by white juries.

JUNE 10

1966

Ben Chester White had been a quiet, familiar presence on the Carter plantation in Natchez for as long as people could remember. The 67-year-old caretaker was a trusted worker and a generous friend. At a time when Mississippi was the center of civil rights turbulence, White was no threat. He never marched or demonstrated. He wasn't even registered to vote. He had no enemies, and there was no reason anyone would want to harm him.

Then a few members of the White Knights of the Ku Klux Klan, calling themselves the Cottonmouth Moccasin Gang, decided to kill a black man. It didn't matter much who they picked; the murder would simply be the lure for a bigger target — Dr. Martin Luther King Jr. At the time, King was leading a mass march through Mississippi to finish a protest begun by James Meredith, who had been wounded by sniper fire earlier in the march. Everywhere King went, he was met by ugly crowds of angry white men. The Natchez Klansmen believed if they could draw King to Natchez, they could assassinate him and make themselves heroes among Klansmen.

The Klansmen decided Ben Chester White would be the lure. One of the Cottonmouth Moccasin Gang, James Jones, remembered gang leader Claude Fuller interrogating White about his views on integration. When Fuller asked, "Don't you feel your children should go to school with whites?" the quiet caretaker nodded in agreement, simply to appease the Klansman. That was all the excuse Fuller needed. He told two other gang members, "He's got to got rid of."

On June 10, 1966, James Jones, Claude Fuller and Ernest Avants picked up White at his home, pretending they needed his help to find a lost dog. Jones drove to a secluded area where they all got out of the car. Fuller aimed his rifle at White and began firing. He emptied one carbine pin and loaded another. This time he pointed the rifle at Avants, and ordered him to shoot into White's bullet-riddled body. Avants fired a shotgun blast that tore apart White's head. The men dumped the remains in a creek and burned the car.

WHAT HAVE I DONE?

A month later, Jones confessed to the crime and was tried for murder. He told the jury he was "deep in sin" and wanted to clear his conscience. He repeated Ben Chester White's final cry: "Oh Lord, what have I done to deserve this?" Nevertheless, the jury could not reach a verdict and Jones was never convicted. A separate jury acquitted Ernest Avants. Although Avants admitted shooting White, he argued he could not be guilty of murder since he had fired into a dead body. Neither Avants nor Jones would agree to testify against Fuller, the man they both said killed White, and Fuller was never tried.

Ben Chester White's son Jesse could not stand to see the killers go unpunished. He filed a civil suit claiming that the Klansmen, under the orders of top White Knights leaders, conspired to violate the civil rights of his father. On November 13, 1968, federal Judge Harold Cox ruled against the Klan, and a jury awarded more than $1 million in damages to White's family. It was the first time a Klan organization was found liable for violence committed by its members. Judge Cox said the award would "serve as a deterrent and message to others who may try to do similar acts."

The verdict gave consolation to another man — Edwin Benoist, the county attorney who had tried unsuccessfully to win murder convictions against the three Klansmen. Twenty-two years after White's death, Benoist still remembered the killing as "the most atrocious murder and the greatest occurrence of injustice" he had ever witnessed. ■

Clarence Triggs was a newcomer to Bogalusa when he joined a civil rights march in early July 1966. He had served in the armed forces and worked as a bricklayer, and had never been very active in the movement. When he moved to Bogalusa with his wife Emma, all he had in mind was his search for a job and a better life. But he could not ignore the injustices he saw.

Triggs had come from Jackson, where Medgar Evers had lost his life in the move to integrate restaurants and downtown businesses. In comparison, Bogalusa was still a Jim Crow town. Not only were blacks kept out of libraries and restaurants because of their race, but they were also segregated on the job. At the Crown-Zellerbach paper mill in Bogalusa where most people worked, black employees were forced to use separate facilities and kept in low-paying jobs. Among the white workers at the mill were a large number of Ku Klux Klan members. In fact, Bogalusa was believed to have more Klan members per capita than any other region of the South in the mid-1960s.

Throughout 1965 and 1966, blacks in Bogalusa staged more than 100 marches for equality in jobs and politics, and tried to protect themselves against the continuing threat of white terrorists. One protest ended in violence when a mob of white men attacked black marchers. At another march, white police officers beat blacks indiscriminately.

Clarence Triggs was one of many blacks in Bogalusa who supported the move for equality by attending the marches and demonstrations, but he was never considered a leader. Few people even knew who he was.

Less than a month after Triggs marched alongside other protesters at a civil rights demonstration, he was found dead next to a car on the side of the road with a bullet wound in his head.

Triggs' murder was never fully explained. One black leader who tried to find out what happened was turned away from the crime scene by police who were investigating. Even Emma Triggs was not allowed to identify her husband's body at the scene.

Believing the police were trying to cover up the murder, civil rights leaders called for nightly marches until there were arrests. Two days later police arrested two white men, Homer Richard Seale and John W. Copling Jr., and charged them with murder. Detectives had found their fingerprints on the steering wheel and a broken Scoth bottle in the car next to Triggs' body. A jury deliberated less than an hour before finding Copling innocent. Seale was never tried.

The motive for Triggs' murder was never revealed, and to this day, his death remains a mystery. ■

Clarence Triggs
(photo unavailable)
1942-1966

Black boycotters who persisted in demanding their equal rights **(left)** inspired Klansmen to retaliate with their own brand of protest **(below)**.

JULY 30

1966

Wharlest Jackson
1929-1967

"Wharlest Jackson had begun to climb out of the darkness into the light, and for this he was cut down."

— Roy Wilkins

For Wharlest Jackson, getting in the car to go to work each day was an act of courage. Jackson, 37, was the treasurer of the local NAACP during a tense period of protests and boycotts by blacks in Natchez. He worked at the Armstrong Rubber Company, where many of the white employees were members of the Ku Klux Klan. When Armstrong officials responded to civil rights demands by opening more jobs to blacks, Wharlest Jackson was offered a promotion to a higher-paying job as mixer of chemicals — a position previously reserved for whites.

Jackson hesitated before accepting the promotion. Word had spread around the plant that blacks who were promoted to "white men's jobs" would not live to enjoy them. These were not idle threats. The local NAACP president, Jackson's friend and co-worker George Metcalfe, was almost killed when a bomb exploded in his car. Jackson, who had worked at the plant for 11 years, knew the risk he was taking when he accepted the promotion. But he needed the extra money for his wife and five children, and he was proud of the opportunity to help demonstrate the achievements of the civil rights movement in Natchez. Mississippi NAACP Field Secretary Charles Evers, who had lost his own brother to assassins, told Jackson his promotion would help pave the way for others.

George Metcalfe gave his friend a word of advice when Jackson took the new job: always check under the hood of your truck before you start it. Metcalfe

had been permanently disabled by the bombing of his own car, and he no longer drove. Instead, he rode to work with Jackson.

On Monday, February 27, 1967, Metcalfe and Jackson were scheduled on separate shifts, so Jackson drove to work alone. He was starting his third week on the new job, and he was full of energy and hope. He told friends that with the 17-cents-an-hour raise, "My wife and children should have a chance now." That night, at 8:01 p.m., Jackson punched the time clock and started for home in a pouring rain. Ten minutes later, a time-delayed bomb which had been planted under the frame of his pickup truck went off, ripping apart the cab and killing Jackson.

after a decade of civil rights murders. The day after Jackson's death, he led 2,000 blacks to the gates of the Armstrong Plant, to "put ourselves before all the Kluxers and say 'You killed our brother, now kill all of us.' " And he hinted that the patience of many blacks was wearing thin. "Once we learn to hate, they're through," he said. "We can kill more people in a day than they've done in 100 years." He threatened a boycott if Armstrong officials did not fire the Klan members on its payroll.

The murder and Evers' stern response spurred white officials into quick action. The Natchez Board of Alderman offered a $25,000 reward for information leading to Jackson's killers, and the Armstrong company added $10,000 to the reward money. The mayor, police chief and sheriff attended a black mass meeting for the first time ever, assuring the community that the case would be vigorously pursued and linking arms at the end of the meeting to join in the civil rights anthem "We Shall Overcome." Mississippi Governor Paul Johnson called the bombing an "act of savagery which stains the honor of our state."

National NAACP Executive Director Roy Wilkins praised city leaders for their response to Jackson's death and said, "Things have changed…throughout the state of Mississippi."

Nevertheless, Jackson's killers were never identified.

Wharlest Jackson was given a military funeral service on March 5, 1967. He had been a Korean War veteran, and his body was placed in a flag-draped casket. At the funeral, Wilkins talked about the long history of racial oppression that had kept American blacks poor and powerless. He said, "Wharlest Jackson had begun to climb out of the darkness into the light, and for this he was cut down." ■

Left. White resistance strengthened as civil rights activities intensified in Mississippi. It took great courage to defy the barriers of racial segregation.
Above. The explosion left Jackson's pickup truck in pieces.

'ACT OF SAVAGERY'

The murder of Wharlest Jackson brought sharp reactions from both blacks and whites in Natchez. Charles Evers, instead of preaching love and forgiveness, gave voice to the bitterness that blacks felt

Benjamin Brown
1945-1967

"Nobody ever came to me and explained why. Nobody, no public official or anything ever came down and said they were sorry my son was killed."

– Ollie Mae Brown

Ben Brown was a child when the Montgomery bus boycott brought the civil rights movement into national focus. He grew up with the spirit of the movement, questioning his parents about the way blacks were treated and eager to learn about the heritage of his race.

By age 16, Ben Brown was an activist. He marched to protest the attacks on the Freedom Riders in 1961. In 1963 he was among thousands who took part in a silent memorial march for the slain civil rights leader Medgar Evers. In high school, he helped organize boycotts against discriminatory businesses. After he graduated, he went to work full time in voter registration.

During the next four years, Brown was harassed, shot at, arrested and jailed for his civil rights activities. His mother, Ollie Mae Brown, urged him to take his talents north where he would be safer, but he refused.

In 1965, Brown was among a thousand protesters who were arrested for picketing Mississippi's all-white state legislature. The protesters were imprisoned at a fairgrounds because the prison could not

hold them. During his incarceration, Brown was walking through a food line when he accidentally dropped his plate into a tank of boiling water. A guard forced him to reach in to retrieve the plate,

and Brown's hand was badly burned.

Threats and abuses did not dampen Brown's spirit for long. He began working for the Delta Ministry, a coalition of Mississippi church groups which worked to combat poverty and discrimination. Brown traveled throughout the poor Delta counties, living on a stipend of $10 a week. He especially enjoyed working with children — he told them stories of famous black figures, taught them games and took them on field trips to the zoo.

By 1966, the intense civil rights activity that characterized Mississippi Freedom Summer had died down, and national civil rights groups were focusing their attention elsewhere. The Delta Ministry, one of the few homegrown civil rights groups in Mississippi, was quickly running out of funds and could no longer pay its workers. Brown saw that it was time to move on in his life.

On the day before Christmas, 1966, Brown married a fellow civil rights worker, Margaret Willis, and by spring they were expecting their first child. Brown worked full time as a truck driver and no longer went to civil rights meetings and demonstrations. To his mother's great relief, he was settling down.

LYNCH STREET

On May 10, 1967, violence erupted on Lynch Street, a short walk from Ben and Margaret's apartment. The trouble began with a student protest against city police actions on Jackson State College campus. The protest grew louder, and non-students from the downtown area joined in. Police sealed off the street with barricades, and some protesters reacted by burning the barricades. The next evening, May 11, city police were joined by state highway patrol and National Guard troops who confronted the protesters with rifles and bayonets.

Toward the end of the second day of protests, Ben Brown walked with a friend into a Lynch Street cafe to pick up a sandwich to take home to Margaret. The cafe was full, so they started down the sidewalk toward another restaurant. Ben had never believed in violent protest and he had not taken part in this one. As he started down Lynch Street, protesters ahead of him began throwing

1967

bricks and bottles at the line of police behind him. One officer was struck with a piece of glass and fired his shotgun into the air. The protesters turned to flee as more policemen opened fire.

Ben and his friend ran when they heard the first gunshot, but Ben was struck by the second round of blasts. He fell to the ground with shotgun wounds in the back of his head and his lower back. A minister who saw the shooting started to help him, but police refused to let anyone near Brown. He lay bleeding on the

her case depended on information contained in the department's own investigative records, which the police refused to release. After nearly 20 years of trying to win justice in the case, she was left with only unanswered questions.

"Nobody ever came to me and explained why," she said. "Nobody, no public official or anything ever came down and said they were sorry my son was killed." ■

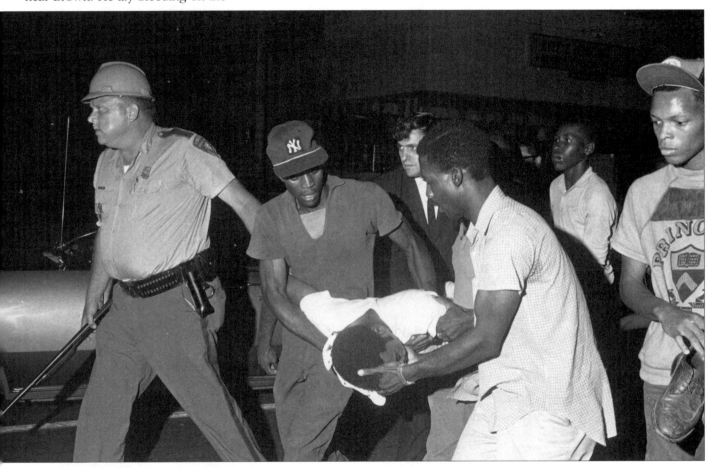

ground for 10 minutes before a National Guard medic came to his aid. It was 45 minutes before an ambulance took him to the hospital. He died early the following morning, his 22nd birthday.

Two other black youths who were shot that night survived. No action was ever taken against the officers who fired their weapons.

Ollie Mae Brown never stopped trying to find out who shot her son. Although eyewitness testimony showed Brown was not among the rioters, and police admitted it was a "wild shot" that killed him, the officer who shot Brown was never identified. Mrs. Brown sued the Jackson police department for the death of her son, but

Opposite page. Ben Brown married fellow civil rights activist Margaret Willis. She was pregnant with their first child when Brown was killed.

Above. Brown is finally carried to an ambulance, after being left bleeding on the street for 45 minutes after he was shot.

Samuel Ephesians Hammond
1949 -1968

Delano Herman Middleton
1950 -1968

Henry Ezekial Smith
1948 -1968

E lizabeth Smith earned $6.40 a day working as a maid for white families in Marion, South Carolina. She raised her four children by herself in a shotgun house in the country, and although she could not afford "luxuries" like indoor plumbing or an automobile, she managed to save money for her one great ambition — to send her children to college.

Henry was her second oldest child. When he went away to South Carolina State College in Orangeburg in the fall of 1966, Henry took with him a strong sense of family responsibility. He wrote home frequently, and called his mother whenever he had a problem he needed to talk about.

On the night of February 6, 1968, Henry called his mother at 2 a.m. He was frustrated and worried. Mrs. Smith listened to his description of what was happening at school, and then urged her son to pray.

That night, Henry Smith was among students who demonstrated at a bowling alley that refused to admit blacks. They were confronted by police with night sticks, and several scuffles erupted. Two women were beaten and many others, including Smith, were injured. The attack on the women enraged Smith, and he complained to his mother that night that student efforts to achieve integration were getting nowhere.

The next day, February 7, students wanted to march downtown to present a list of grievances to city officials, but their parade permit was denied. Tensions ran high. That night, the bowling alley was closed and the National Guard was called in, but there was no violence.

The next night, still barred from the bowling alley and surrounded by police, students began to look for an outlet for their anger. Henry Smith was with about 200 students who gathered around a bonfire on a campus street. They were matched by an equal number of highway patrolmen, National Guardsmen, police

officers and sheriff's deputies. The police put out the fire, and some students retaliated by throwing rocks and bottles. Students rebuilt the bonfire and police again arrived to put it out. This time someone struck a patrolman with a bannister post pulled from a vacant house. More objects were thrown. A shot rang out, and students started to run away. Then a volley of shotgun blasts were fired from police into the retreating crowd.

THE VICTIMS

Henry Smith was one of the first to fall. He was shot five times in the sides

and back. Delano Middleton, a 17-year-old high school student whose mother worked as a maid at the college, was shot three times in the forearm, once in the hip, and also in the thigh, the side of the chest, and the heart. Samuel Hammond, a football player from Fort Lauderdale, Florida, was shot once in the back. Within ten seconds, 27 students had been struck by shotgun fire — most had multiple wounds and all but three were hit from the rear or the side. Many were shot in the feet as they lay on the ground.

Samuel Hammond died less than an

hour after the shooting. The stocky 18-year-old had lettered in track and football at a newly integrated high school in Fort Lauderdale, and had come to State College with the ambition of becoming a teacher. A white high school teammate, John Bogert, heard about the tragedy at Orangeburg and wrote a letter to the Fort Lauderdale paper. He remembered Hammond as a loyal friend and mature competitor, and wrote, "This incident has caused me to take a long hard look at what I believe to be true. How could I say that what Sam died for is wrong?…I can only sit here and look at the news photo which was taken while I stood next to him at Lockhart Stadium and feel, as another student once put it, that someone had killed my brother."

Delano Middleton's mother made it to her son's hospital bedside in time to hear him describe the "bullets…flying everywhere." Delano's main interests were church and sports, and he had never been involved in civil rights activities. He had gone to the campus that night simply out of curiosity. As he realized he was dying, Delano asked his mother to recite the Twenty-third Psalm. "The Lord is My Shepherd," she began. He repeated it with her, then he died.

The doctors thought they had a chance to save Henry Smith, but his wounds suddenly hemorrhaged and he passed away a half hour after Middleton.

KILLER SHOT

The first news stories described the violence on campus as a gun battle between students and patrolmen. Law enforcement and government officials immediately blamed the tragedy on black militants.

Later investigations proved that the students in fact did not have guns and no one but patrolmen had fired weapons on the night of February 8. The evidence also showed that patrolmen shot at random into a retreating crowd — there was no attacking mob. The patrolmen did not follow accepted riot control procedures. Instead of using tear gas or less powerful ammunition against the disruptive students, the patrolmen fired deadly buckshot.

Despite the evidence, a grand jury in October 1968 failed to indict the officers who fired their guns. Six months later, the U.S. Justice Department brought federal charges against nine highway patrolmen for using excessive force against the students. All nine were acquitted.

The Attorney General of the United States, Ramsey Clark, disputed the general opinion that the officers had acted appropriately. "To use double-ought buckshot — it's a killer shot. You use it when you're trying to kill somebody. To think that law enforcement had to try to kill somebody to contain those students is to think wrongly. That cannot be true.

"You wonder if this had been Clemson or Amherst or Princeton or some place like that, what the public reaction would have been," Clark said.

Still, state and local officials never acknowledged that mistakes were made in handling the Orangeburg protesters.

Two days after the shootings, the Justice Department filed suit to integrate the bowling alley. State bond issues were passed later that year to make improvements at the college. A year after the killings, a new physical education building on campus was dedicated as the Smith-Hammond-Middleton Memorial Center. A granite marker was placed on campus to honor the three students who lost their lives "in pursuit of human dignity." And each year, Samuel Hammond, Delano Middleton, and Henry Smith are honored at a memorial service, as the victims of what has become known as the Orangeburg Massacre. ■

Opposite page. Firemen douse the bonfire built by student protesters at South Carolina State College.
Above. Henry Smith (left) and Delano Middleton lie wounded on the sidewalk after being shot by highway patrolmen.

**Martin Luther
King Jr.**
1929 -1968

When black leaders in Montgomery launched a boycott of city buses in December 1955, they picked an articulate young newcomer as their spokesman. Martin Luther King Jr. was the minister of Dexter Avenue Baptist Church, the son of a prominent Atlanta preacher, and a biblical scholar who received his doctorate at age 26 from Boston University School of Theology.

King had a coolness about him when he discussed ideas and strategy, but his preaching could set a congregation on fire. The first night of the boycott, King spoke to a mass meeting at Holt Street Baptist Church in Montgomery. He told the boycotters they had truth on their side, and made them believe they could win the bat-

tle for equality. "One of the great glories of democracy is the right to protest for right," he said.

King told them they were right to be tired of discrimination and injustice. "For many years, we have shown amazing patience…But we come here tonight to be saved from that patience that makes us patient with anything less than freedom and justice." By the time King finished his remarks, the boycotters were jubilant in the face of their challenge.

King's calm under pressure and his transcendent rhetoric sustained the Montgomery bus boycotters through 13 months and made King the most influential figure of the entire civil rights era. Through the next 13 years, he would not only lead a

major social revolution but would inspire a transformation of conscience in America.

Martin Luther King's life was in danger from the moment his enemies recognized the power he held. Klansmen bombed his home in Montgomery. He was attacked by fanatical white supremacists in Selma, and stabbed by an angry black woman in New York. He spent many nights alone in jail. He received countless death threats.

In spite of the danger, he continued to lead campaigns for integration — in Albany in 1962, in Birmingham in 1963, in St. Augustine in 1964, and in Selma in 1965. He led with an imagination and strength that surprised his friends as well as his enemies.

In Birmingham, he wrote a letter from his jail cell answering the criticism of moderate clergy who thought he was demanding too much too soon. "For years now I have heard the words 'Wait!' It rings in the ear of every Negro with a piercing familiarity. This 'wait!' has almost always meant

'Never!'…We have waited for more than 340 years for our constitutional and God-given rights…There comes a time when the cup of endurance runs over."

In Selma, he issued a nationwide call for clergy to come South for the march to Montgomery. Within two days, hundreds of people poured into Alabama with little more than the clothes on their backs, thrilled just to be marching with Dr. King.

Through him, the doctrine of nonviolence became the movement's unifying

Left. Montgomery police take King into custody.
Opposite page and below.
Though he was a calm strategist, King became famous for his intense oratory.

philosophy. Over and over, King preached the difficult message of peaceful confrontation. Demand your rights, he urged, but love your enemies.

When the movement suffered setbacks and tragedy, like the Birmingham church bombing and the death of Jimmie Lee Jackson, King comforted his followers by reminding them that "undeserved suffering does not go unredeemed." Love, he preached, would conquer hatred.

It was King who brought the movement to its highest emotional peak, during the March on Washington on August 28, 1963. "I have a dream," he told the crowd of 250,000 who gathered in front of the Lincoln Memorial. "It is a dream deeply

rooted in the American dream, that one day this nation will rise up and live out the true meaning of its creed — we hold these truths to be self-evident, that all men are created equal."

His gift of rhetoric and his personal strength enabled King to rise above the divisions that plagued civil rights groups in the mid-60s and to withstand the criticism of political leaders as well as the constant

scrutiny of J. Edgar Hoover's FBI. His strong spiritual focus led King to address the issues of world peace and poverty in the years before his death. He spoke out against the Vietnam War and launched anti-poverty campaigns in Chicago and

Cleveland. He had gone to Memphis to support a sanitation workers' strike for fair wages when he was assassinated.

King died a hero to many people of all colors throughout the world. He provided a model for successful social change that today inspires blacks living in South Africa and people everywhere who are denied their rights.

A Nobel Peace Prize winner, King asked not to be remembered for his awards but for his character. Two months before he was killed, he told a congregation in Atlanta that when he died, he wanted only for "somebody to mention that day, that Martin Luther King Jr. tried to give his life serving others."

Nine years after his death, Martin Luther King Jr. was awarded the Presidential Medal of Freedom. The citation reads, in part:

"Martin Luther King Jr. was the conscience of his generation. A Southerner, a black man, he gazed on the great wall of segregation and saw that the power of love could bring it down...He helped us overcome our ignorance of one another...He made our nation stronger because he made it better...

"His life informed us, his dreams sustain us yet." ■

Opposite page. King delivering his "I Have a Dream Speech" during the March on Washington.
Top. King with his father (left), wife Coretta and their children.
Above. King leads off the last leg of the Selma to Montgomery march.

Civil Rights Tim

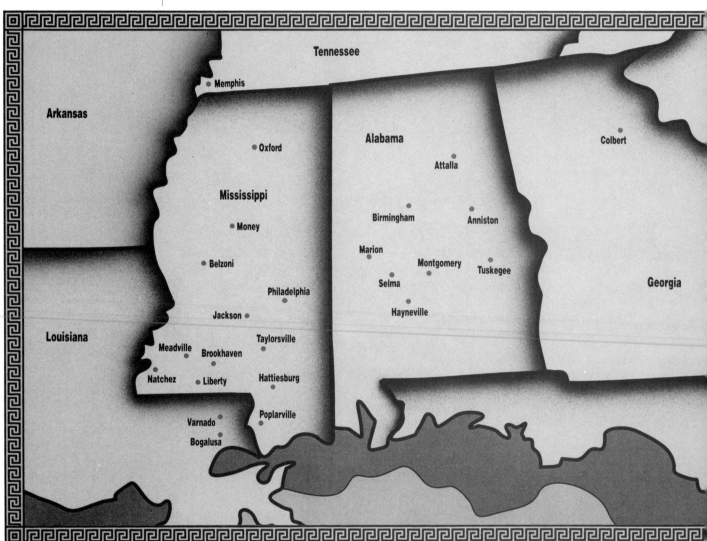

17 • MAY • 1954
SUPREME COURT OUTLAWS SCHOOL SEGREGATION IN BROWN VS. BOARD OF EDUCATION

7 • MAY • 1955
REV. GEORGE LEE • KILLED FOR LEADING VOTER REGISTRATION DRIVE • BELZONI, MS

13 • AUG • 1955
LAMAR SMITH • MURDERED FOR ORGANIZING BLACK VOTERS • BROOKHAVEN, MS

28 • AUG • 1955
EMMETT LOUIS TILL • YOUTH MURDERED FOR SPEAKING TO WHITE WOMAN • MONEY, MS

22 • OCT • 1955
JOHN EARL REESE • SLAIN BY NIGHTRIDERS OPPOSED TO BLACK SCHOOL IMPROVEMENTS • MAYFLOWER, TX

1 • DEC • 1955
ROSA PARKS ARRESTED FOR REFUSING TO GIVE UP HER SEAT ON BUS TO A WHITE MAN • MONTGOMERY, AL

Orangeburg

eline

23 • JAN • 1957
WILLIE EDWARDS JR. • KILLED BY KLAN • MONTGOMERY, AL

29 • AUG • 1957
CONGRESS PASSES FIRST CIVIL RIGHTS ACT SINCE RECONSTRUCTION

24 • SEP • 1957
PRESIDENT EISENHOWER ORDERS FEDERAL TROOPS TO ENFORCE SCHOOL DESEGREGATION • LITTLE ROCK, AR

25 • APR • 1959
MACK CHARLES PARKER • TAKEN FROM JAIL AND LYNCHED • POPLARVILLE, MS

1 • FEB • 1960
BLACK STUDENTS STAGE SIT-IN AT 'WHITES ONLY' LUNCH COUNTER • GREENSBORO, NC

5 • DEC • 1960
SUPREME COURT OUTLAWS SEGREGATION IN BUS TERMINALS

14 • MAY • 1961
FREEDOM RIDERS ATTACKED IN ALABAMA WHILE TESTING COMPLIANCE WITH BUS DESEGREGATION LAWS

25 • SEP • 1961
HERBERT LEE • VOTER REGISTRATION WORKER KILLED BY WHITE LEGISLATOR • LIBERTY, MS

1 • APR • 1962
CIVIL RIGHTS GROUPS JOIN FORCES TO LAUNCH VOTER REGISTRATION DRIVE

9 • APR • 1962
CPL. ROMAN DUCKSWORTH JR. • TAKEN FROM BUS AND KILLED BY POLICE • TAYLORSVILLE, MS

30 • SEP • 1962
RIOTS ERUPT WHEN JAMES MEREDITH, A BLACK STUDENT, ENROLLS AT OLE MISS

30 • SEP • 1962
PAUL GUIHARD • EUROPEAN REPORTER KILLED DURING OLE MISS RIOT • OXFORD, MS

23 • APR • 1963
WILLIAM LEWIS MOORE • SLAIN DURING ONE-MAN MARCH AGAINST SEGREGATION • ATTALLA, AL

3 • MAY • 1963
BIRMINGHAM POLICE ATTACK MARCHING CHILDREN WITH DOGS AND FIRE HOSES

11 • JUN • 1963
ALABAMA GOVERNOR STANDS IN SCHOOLHOUSE DOOR TO STOP UNIVERSITY INTEGRATION

12 • JUN • 1963
MEDGAR EVERS • CIVIL RIGHTS LEADER ASSASSINATED • JACKSON, MS

28 • AUG • 1963
250,000 AMERICANS MARCH ON WASHINGTON FOR CIVIL RIGHTS

15 • SEP • 1963
ADDIE MAE COLLINS • DENISE MCNAIR • CAROLE ROBERTSON • CYNTHIA WESLEY • SCHOOLGIRLS KILLED IN BOMBING OF 16TH ST. BAPTIST CHURCH • BIRMINGHAM, AL

5 • DEC • 1955
MONTGOMERY BUS BOYCOTT BEGINS

13 • NOV • 1956
SUPREME COURT BANS SEGREGATED SEATING ON MONTGOMERY BUSES

The names of those who died and the major events of the movement are engraved in the Civil Rights Memorial in Montgomery, Alabama.

I don't know what will happen now. We've got some difficult days ahead. But it doesn't matter with me now. Because I've been to the mountaintop...I've seen the promised land. I may not get there with you. But I want you to know tonight, that we, as a people will get to the promised land.

—Martin Luther King Jr.
April 3, 1968
Memphis, Tennessee

15 • SEP • 1963
VIRGIL LAMAR WARE • YOUTH KILLED DURING WAVE OF RACIST VIOLENCE • BIRMINGHAM, AL

23 • JAN • 1964
POLL TAX OUTLAWED IN FEDERAL ELECTIONS

31 • JAN • 1964
LOUIS ALLEN • WITNESS TO MURDER OF CIVIL RIGHTS WORKER, ASSASSINATED • LIBERTY, MS

7 • APR • 1964
REV. BRUCE KLUNDER • KILLED PROTESTING CONSTRUCTION OF SEGREGATED SCHOOL • CLEVELAND, OH

2 • MAY • 1964
HENRY HEZEKIAH DEE • CHARLES EDDIE MOORE • KILLED BY KLAN • MEADVILLE, MS

20 • JUN • 1964
FREEDOM SUMMER BRINGS 1,000 YOUNG CIVIL RIGHTS VOLUNTEERS TO MISSISSIPPI

21 • JUN • 1964
JAMES CHANEY • ANDREW GOODMAN • MICHAEL SCHWERNER • CIVIL RIGHTS WORKERS ABDUCTED AND SLAIN BY KLAN • PHILADELPHIA, MS

2 • JUL • 1964
PRESIDENT JOHNSON SIGNS CIVIL RIGHTS ACT OF 1964

11 • JUL • 1964
LT. COL. LEMUEL PENN • KILLED BY KLAN WHILE DRIVING NORTH • COLBERT, GA

26 • FEB • 1965
JIMMIE LEE JACKSON • CIVIL RIGHTS MARCHER KILLED BY STATE TROOPER • MARION, AL

7 • MAR • 1965
STATE TROOPERS BEAT BACK MARCHERS AT EDMUND PETTUS BRIDGE • SELMA, AL

11 • MAR • 1965
REV. JAMES REEB • MARCH VOLUNTEER BEATEN TO DEATH • SELMA, AL

25 • MAR • 1965
CIVIL RIGHTS MARCH FROM SELMA TO MONTGOMERY COMPLETED

25 • MAR • 1965
VIOLA GREGG LIUZZO • KILLED BY KLAN WHILE TRANSPORTING MARCHERS • SELMA HIGHWAY, AL

2 • JUN • 1965
ONEAL MOORE • BLACK DEPUTY KILLED BY NIGHTRIDERS • VARNADO, LA

9 • JULY • 1965
CONGRESS PASSES VOTING RIGHTS ACT OF 1965

18 • JUL • 1965
WILLIE WALLACE BREWSTER • KILLED BY NIGHTRIDERS • ANNISTON, AL

20 • AUG • 1965
JONATHAN DANIELS • SEMINARY STUDENT KILLED BY DEPUTY • HAYNEVILLE, AL

3 • JAN • 1966
SAMUEL YOUNGE JR. • STUDENT CIVIL RIGHTS ACTIVIST KILLED IN DISPUTE OVER WHITES-ONLY RESTROOM • TUSKEGEE, AL

10 • JAN • 1966
VERNON DAHMER • BLACK COMMUNITY LEADER KILLED IN KLAN BOMBING • HATTIESBURG, MS

10 • JUN • 1966
BEN CHESTER WHITE • KILLED BY KLAN • NATCHEZ, MS

30 • JUL • 1966
CLARENCE TRIGGS • SLAIN BY NIGHTRIDERS • BOGALUSA, LA

27 • FEB • 1967
WHARLEST JACKSON • CIVIL RIGHTS LEADER KILLED AFTER PROMOTION TO 'WHITE' JOB • NATCHEZ, MS

12 • MAY • 1967
BENJAMIN BROWN • CIVIL RIGHTS WORKER KILLED WHEN POLICE FIRED ON PROTESTERS • JACKSON, MS

2 • OCT • 1967
THURGOOD MARSHALL SWORN IN AS FIRST BLACK SUPREME COURT JUSTICE

8 • FEB • 1968
SAMUEL HAMMOND JR. • DELANO MIDDLETON • HENRY SMITH • STUDENTS KILLED WHEN HIGHWAY PATROLMEN FIRED ON PROTESTERS • ORANGEBURG, SC

4 • APR • 1968
DR. MARTIN LUTHER KING JR. • ASSASSINATED • MEMPHIS, TN

The Civil Rights Memorial

...UNTIL JUSTICE ROLLS DOWN LIKE WATERS AND RIGHTEOUSNESS LIKE A MIGHTY STREAM

The Civil Rights Memorial was built in 1989 by the Southern Poverty Law Center in Montgomery, Alabama, as part of an ongoing effort to educate young people about the civil rights movement and the continuing problems of intolerance in America.

Maya Lin, who also designed the Vietnam Veterans Memorial in Washington, D.C., sought a design for the Civil Rights Memorial which would not only honor movement heroes, but would become a vehicle for education and reflection.

The memorial includes a black granite table engraved with names of those who died during the movement as well as key events of the period. Over the table flows a thin sheet of water which glistens with light and reflects the image of the viewer.

The Memorial, Maya Lin says, is "a place to remember the civil rights movement, to honor those killed during the struggle, to appreciate how far the country has come in its quest for equality, and to consider how far it has to go."

...to appreciate how far the country has come in its quest for equality, and to consider how far it has to go.

Teaching Tolerance

The book you are reading was produced by Teaching Tolerance, the education project of the Southern Poverty Law Center. A magazine version of *Free at Last* is part of a complete curriculum package called *America's Civil Rights Movement,* which also includes an award-winning 38-minute video documentary as well as a teacher's guide with lesson plans. *America's Civil Rights Movement* is available free to schools upon request of the principal. (Limit: one package per school.)

Teaching Tolerance also publishes and distributes free to teachers a semiannual magazine called *Teaching Tolerance* that offers ideas, resources and models for promoting interracial and intercultural understanding in the classroom.

For more information, write to:

Teaching Tolerance
400 Washington Ave.
Montgomery, AL 36104
FAX 205/264-0629

TEACHING
TOLERANCE

Spring/92

Further Readin

Black history—general

Bennett, Lerone. *Before the Mayflower: A History of Black America*. Rev. ed. New York: Viking Penguin, 1984.

Berry, Mary Frances, and John W. Blassingame. *Long Memory: The Black Experience in America*. New York: Oxford University Press, 1982.

Franklin, John Hope, and August Meier, eds. *Black Leaders of the Twentieth Century*. Urbana: University of Illinois Press, 1982.

Franklin, John Hope, and Alfred A. Moss, Jr. *From Slavery to Freedom: A History of Negro Americans*. 6th ed. New York: Knopf, 1987.

Lincoln, C. Eric, and Lawrence H. Mamiya. *The Black Church in the African American Experience*. Durham, N.C.: Duke University Press, 1990.

Meltzer, Milton. *The Black Americans: A History in Their Own Words, 1619-1983*. New York: HarperCollins, 1984.

Myers, Walter D. *Now Is Your Time! The African-American Struggle for Freedom*. New York: HarperCollins, 1991.

Quarles, Benjamin. *The Negro in the Making of America*. 3rd ed., rev. New York: Collier, 1987.

Civil rights movement

Blumberg, Rhoda L. *Civil Rights: The 1960s Freedom Struggle*. Boston: Twayne, 1984.

Branch, Taylor. *Parting the Waters: America in the King Years, 1954-63*. New York: Simon & Schuster, 1988.

Cagin, Seth, and Philip Dray. *We Are Not Afraid: The Story of Goodman, Schwerner & Chaney and the Civil Rights Campaign for Mississippi*. New York: Bantam, 1991.

Carson, Clayborne, et al. *The Eyes on the Prize Civil Rights Reader: Documents, Speeches, and Firsthand Accounts from the Black Freedom Struggle, 1954-1990*. New York: Viking, 1991.

Durham, Michael S. *Powerful Days: The Civil Rights Photography of Charles Moore*. New York: Stewart Tabori & Chang, 1991.

Fager, Charles E. *Selma 1965: The March That Changed the South*. New York: Scribners, 1974.

Graham, Hugh Davis. *The Civil Rights Era: Origins and Development of National Policy, 1960-72*. New York: Oxford University Press, 1990.

Hampton, Henry, and Steve Fayer. *Voices of Freedom: An Oral History of the Civil Rights Movement from the 1950s through the 1980s*. New York: Bantam, 1990.

Kosof, Anna. *The Civil Rights Movement and Its Legacy*. New York: Franklin Watts, 1989.

McAdam, Doug. *Freedom Summer*. New York: Oxford University Press, 1988.

McKissack, Patricia and Floyd McKissack. *The Civil Rights Movement in America From 1865 to the Present*. 2nd ed. Chicago: Childrens Press, 1987.

Moody, Anne. *Coming of Age in Mississippi*. New York: Dell, 1968.

Raines, Howell. *My Soul Is Rested: Movement Days in the Deep South Remembered*. New York: Putnam, 1977.

Seeger, Pete, and Robert S. Reiser. *Everybody Says Freedom: The Civil Rights Movement in Words, Pictures & Song*. New York: Norton, 1990.

Williams, Juan. *Eyes on the Prize: America's Civil Rights Years, 1954-65*. New York: Viking, 1987.

Youth of the Rural Organizing and Cultural Center. *Minds Stayed on Freedom: The Civil Rights Struggle in the Rural South, an Oral History*. Boulder, Colo.: Westview, 1991.

Martin Luther King, Jr.

Garrow, David J. *Bearing the Cross: Martin Luther King, Jr., and the Southern Christian Leadership Conference.* New York: Morrow, 1986.

Jakoubek, Robert. *Martin Luther King, Jr.* Introduction by Coretta Scott King. New York: Chelsea House, 1990.

King, Coretta Scott. *My Life with Martin Luther King, Jr.* New York: Holt, Rinehart & Winston, 1979.

King, Martin Luther, Jr. *Stride Toward Freedom: A Leader of His People Tells the Montgomery Story.* New York: Harper, 1958.

———. *A Testament of Hope: The Essential Writings of Martin Luther King, Jr.* ed. James M. Washington. San Francisco: Harper & Row, 1986.

——— *Why We Can't Wait.* New York: NAL, 1964.

Patterson, Lillie. *Martin Luther King, Jr. and the Freedom Movement.* New York: Facts on File, 1989.

Schulke, Flip. *Martin Luther King, Jr. A Documentary... From Montgomery to Memphis.* Introduction by Coretta Scott King. New York: Norton, 1976.

Other Biographies and Autobiographies

Aldred, Lisa. *Thurgood Marshall.* New York: Chelsea House, 1990.

Farmer, James. *Freedom— When?* New York: Random House, 1965.

———. *Lay Bare the Heart: The Autobiography of the Civil Rights Movement.* New York: Arbor House, 1985.

King, Martin Luther, Sr. *Daddy King: An Autobiography.* New York: Morrow, 1980.

Parks, Rosa, with Jim Haskins. *Rosa Parks: My Story.* New York: Dial, 1992.

Smead, Howard. *Blood Justice: The Lynching of Mack Charles Parker.* New York: Oxford University Press, 1988.

Webb, Sheyann, and Rachel West Nelson, as told to Frank Sikora. *Selma, Lord, Selma: Girlhood Memories of the Civil Rights Days.* Tuscaloosa: University of Alabama Press, 1980.

The Civil Rights Memorial

Bullard, Sara. "Martyrs of the Movement: Forty Who Died in the Civil Rights Struggle." *American Visions,* February 1990 p. 36.

Cheers, D. Michael. "Dedicate memorial to 40 who died in civil rights struggle." *Jet,* November 20, 1989, p. 4.

Coleman, Jonathan. "First she looks inward: architect Maya Lin's Viet Nam memorial proved to be a powerful emotional reminder. Now she has created another." *Time,* November 5, 1989, p. 90.

"A memorial to civil rights." *Southern Living,* February 1991, p. 24.

Stein, Karen. "Touch Stone." *Architectural Record,* February 1990, p. 186.

Zinsser, William. "I realized her tears were becoming part of the memorial." *Smithsonian,* September 1991, p. 32.

Index

Credits

Cover: Martin Luther King, Jr.: Black Star; demonstration: © Bruce Davidson/Magnum

p. 3: Mark Wright

p. 6: Fred Powledge

p. 7: courtesy Julian Bond

p. 8 top left: Matt Herron/Black Star

p. 9 left: © Bob Adelman/Magnum Photos

p. 10, 11, 12 (all photos): The Bettmann Archive

p. 13: UPI/Bettmann Newsphotos

p. 14: UPI/Bettmann Newsphotos

p. 15: Library of Congress

p. 16: UPI/Bettmann Newsphotos

p. 17: Roger Malloch/Black Star

p. 18: Flip Schulke/Black Star

p. 19 top: Charles Moore/Black Star

p. 19 bottom: UPI/Bettmann Newsphotos

p. 20 top: UPI/Bettmann Newsphotos

pp. 20-21 bottom:Steve Schapiro/Black Star

p. 21 top and right: UPI/Bettmann Newsphotos

pp. 22-23: Bruce Roberts

p. 24 top and bottom: UPI/Bettmann Newsphotos

p. 25: © Bruce Davidson/Magnum Photos

p. 26, 27 (all photos): Charles Moore/Black Star

p. 28: © Bob Henriques/Magnum Photos

p. 29: Fred Ward/Black Star

p. 30 left: Bob Fitch/Black Star

pp. 30-31 top: Charles Moore/Black Star

p. 31 right: Black Star

p. 32 left: Charles Moore/Black Star

p. 32 center: © Danny Lyon/Magnum Photos

p. 33: Steve Schapiro/Black Star

p. 34 top: © Bob Adelman/Magnum Photos

p. 34 right: UPI/Bettmann Newsphotos

p. 35 top: UPI/Bettmann Newsphotos

p. 35 right: © Bruce Davidson/Magnum Photos

p. 35 bottom: © Bob Adelman/Magnum Photos

p. 36: Ron McCool/Black Star

p. 37: UPI/Bettmann Newsphotos

p. 38: Declan Haun/Black Star

p. 39 top: © Eli Reed/Magnum Photos

p. 39 bottom: © Bruce Davidson/Magnum Photos

p. 41: © Eve Arnold/Magnum Photos

pp. 42-43 bottom: Bob Fitch/Black Star

pp. 44, 45 (all photos): UPI/Bettmann Newsphotos

p. 46: © Bruce Davidson/Magnum Photos

p. 49, 50, 51 (all photos): UPI/Bettmann Newsphotos

p. 53: © Danny Lyon/Magnum Photos

p. 54: Lee Lockwood/Black Star

p. 55: UPI/Bettmann Newsphotos

p. 56 top left: UPI/Bettmann Newsphotos

p. 56 center: Charles Moore/Black Star

p. 57 both photos: Flip Schulke/Black Star

p. 58: courtesy Mary Moore Birchard

p. 59: © Bob Adelman/Magnum Photos

p. 60 left: Black Star

p. 60 right: Flip Schulke/Black Star

p. 61: UPI/Bettmann Newsphotos

p. 62 and 63 (four girls): Birmingham News

p. 62 right: UPI/Bettmann Newsphotos

p. 63 left: UPI/Bettmann Newsphotos

p. 65: Charles Moore/Black Star

p. 67: © Bruce Davidson/Magnum Photos

p. 68, 69, 70 (all photos): UPI/Bettmann Newsphotos

p. 71 top: Steve Schapiro/Black Star

p. 71 bottom: Bill Reed/Black Star

p. 72: Vernon Meritt III/Black Star

p. 73, 75: UPI/Bettmann Newsphotos

p. 76 right: UPI/Bettmann Newsphotos

p. 77: UPI/Bettmann Newsphotos

p. 78: UPI/Bettmann Newsphotos

p. 79: Charles Moore/Black Star

p. 80 right: © Bruce Davidson/Magnum Photos

p. 81 top: UPI/Bettmann Newsphotos

p. 81 bottom: © Bruce Davidson/Magnum Photos

p. 82, 83: UPI/Bettmann Newsphotos

p. 84, 85, 86, 87, 89: UPI/Bettmann Newsphotos

p. 90, 91: AP/Wide World Photos

p. 92 center; Matt Herron/Black Star

p. 93 top: Billy E. Barnes/Black Star

p. 93 bottom: © Danny Lyon/Magnum Photos

p. 94 top left: AP/Wide World Photos

p. 94 right: Steve Schapiro/Black Star

p. 95 top: UPI/Bettmann Newsphotos

p. 96 : courtesy Mrs. Ollie Mae Brown

p. 97: UPI/Bettmann Newsphotos

p. 98 left colum: Cecil J. Williams

p. 100 top left: © Bruce Davidson/Magnum Photos

p. 100 center and right: Flip Schulke/Black Star

p. 101 bottom left and right: Flip Schulke/Black Star

p. 101 top: Charles Moore/Black Star

p. 102: Flip Schulke/Black Star

p. 103 top: Black Star

p. 103 bottom: UPI/Bettmann Newsphotos

p. 104: illustration by Daniel Armstrong

p. 108: John O'Hagan

back cover: Matt Herron/Black Star

Sara Bullard is editor of *Teaching Tolerance,* a national educational magazine, and director of education for the Southern Poverty Law Center in Montgomery, Alabama. After graduating from the University of North Carolina, Ms. Bullard worked as a feature and investigative journalist in Fort Lauderdale, Baltimore, and Boston. In 1985 she joined the staff of the North Carolina Human Relations Council, where she investigated employment and housing discrimination and white supremacist activities. In 1986 she joined the SPLC, where she researched and wrote the bimonthly *Klanwatch Intelligence Report* and such special publications as *The Ku Klux Klan: A Legacy of Hate and Violence.* When the SPLC sponsored the construction of the Civil Rights Memorial in 1989, she was responsible, in conjunction with an advisory board of civil rights leaders, for identifying the people whose names are on the memorial. Ms. Bullard has also published articles in *Educational Leadership, American Visions, The New York Times,* and many other publications, and her fiction has appeared in *Southern Humanities Review.*

Julian Bond has been an active participant in the civil rights movement since his student days at Morehouse College. In 1960 he was a founder of the Committee on Appeal for Human Rights (COHAR), the Atlanta University Center student civil rights organization that directed three years of non-voiolent anti-segregation protests and won integration of Atlanta's movie theatres, lunch counters, and parks. He helped form the Student Nonviolent Coordinating Committee (SNCC) in 1960 and served as its communications director. Mr. Bond went on to serve four terms in the Georgia House of Representatives and six terms in the state Senate. The host of "America's Black Forum," the oldest black-owned show in television syndication, he is the author of *A Time To Speak, A Time to Act* and *Black Candidates— Southern Campaign Experiences.* Mr. Bond is currently a Distinguished Scholar in Residence at American University in Washington, D.C. and a visiting professor at Williams College.

FRANKLIN PIERCE COLLEGE LIBRARY

00081954